A WINTER'S TALE

5/30

A
WINTER'S
TALE

Fraser Harrison

Illustrated by Harriet Dell

Flamingo
Published by Fontana Paperbacks

First published in Great Britain by
William Collins Sons & Co. Ltd 1987

This Flamingo edition first published
in 1988 by Fontana Paperbacks,
8 Grafton Street, London W1X 3LA

Flamingo is an imprint of
Fontana Paperbacks, part of
the Collins Publishing Group

Printed and bound in Great Britain by
William Collins Sons & Co. Ltd, Glasgow

CONTENTS

PROLOGUE

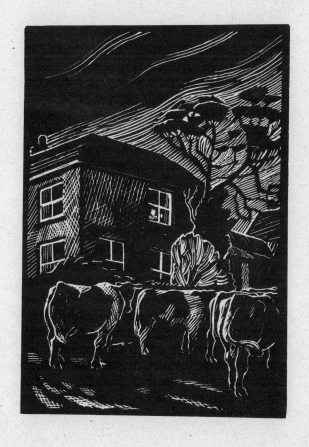

Exactly three years ago I made the last entry in the journal which was published later as *A Father's Diary* (Flamingo, 1985). This was a day-to-day record of a year in the life of a father and his two children. As such, it turned out to be an unusual document; for it is one of the curiosities of our literature that whereas innumerable portraits exist of fathers depicted by vengeful sons, a rogues' gallery now being added to by daughters' portraits of their monstrous mothers, there are next to no descriptions of ordinary children written on the spot by ordinary parents.

Over the last fifteen or so years the rigours, if not the rewards, of motherhood have been extensively written about, but fatherhood, while no longer the neglected topic it used to be, has remained more or less the monopoly of psychologists and sociologists. All writers write out of their own experience, some more directly and overtly than others, and as far as I am concerned the most important and influential experience of my recent life has been the existence of my children. Their impact on me and my marriage, the phenomenon of their development, to say nothing of their singular and delightful characters, have been the centre to which my thoughts and feelings have been continually drawn ever since I wrote the words, 'Sally pregnant. Hurrah!' in an earlier diary. As soon as I finished my account of a father's year, there was nothing I wanted to do more than write about the children again. However, I did not want to set up business as a professional father; still less did I want to pose as an expert or, worse, as a dispenser of advice. As this present book demonstrates all too graphically, I am still struggling ineptly with my own experience as a father and husband, and have no confidence in anything but my ability to tell my own story.

Apart from a natural reluctance to perform the same trick twice, I did not want to write another diary because I thought it unfair to the children, who were of course growing older and more aware by the day, to expose them once again to public gaze, and I did not relish casting myself in the role of spy in my own family. In any case, there were issues and events I wanted to discuss which would not have been comfortably embraced by another diary written, as it were, on the run. Like anyone who is artistically preoccupied by children, I knew I was partly engaged on a quest for my own childhood self.

Despite my close observation of the children over a whole year, at the end of it I was left with the conviction that there was something mysterious about childhood, an impalpable dimension which I had failed to penetrate. Added to this, I could not reconcile the opaque and scrappy impression I had retained of my own childhood with the almost frightening intensity of absorption in every tiny, passing event which all children seem to enjoy. Why had my own, presumably no less intense responses left so little trace in adult consciousness? I would watch my children as they played some commonplace game, or were enthralled by some treat, the kind of games and treats I had known as a child, and wonder whether their utterly exclusive engagement in them was destined to evaporate, leaving barely any mark on their memory, as it had done in my case. Was I exceptional in this? Were my powers of recall unusually weak, or were they the victims of an inhibiting force I could not identify? Or, was this obliteration of memory

4

simply an ordinary function of childhood?

Childhood is bound to be something of a mystery since it is undergone by people who lack the expressive ability, and the inclination, to report back. The mystery is further compounded by the fact that it is recalled by adults who are only distantly related to their child-selves, and who seem to suffer from a restraint of memory which is not lifted until old age. Biology is, presumably, playing a part here: the child's personality could hardly grow if it were burdened with an adult's powers of self-reflection, and by the same token adulthood would be intolerable, would indeed be a state of madness, if it retained childhood's raw and helpless exposure to feeling.

I am sure my concern with the inscrutable nature of childhood was exaggerated because I felt so disconnected from my own. Parents who have the keenest intuition of their children's imaginative life are probably those who have preserved a sharply focused impression of themselves as children, making it easy for them to identify with their children's feelings and reactions, even when these are enigmatically expressed. Though I am close to my children, I do not believe that I am unusually sensitive to what they think and feel: I observe carefully, but do not always understand clearly. I attribute this failing in part to having only the most scattered and vague recollections of my childhood self and history.

While thinking about all this I read two splendid childhood autobiograpies, Edward Blishen's *Sorry, Dad* and George Melly's *Scouse Mouse*, and was amazed by their almost supernatural ability to recreate the fine detail of their homes, families and the narrative of their earliest years. Every doorknob and Christmas joke, every sea-shell and toy soldier, seems to have been kept in their minds in a state of pristine brilliance. This comprehensiveness of recall is presumably a gift, which no amount of literary straining will replace. It must also be the product of a free-flowing reconciliation with one's past and, most significantly, one's parents; perhaps such books can only be written after one's parents are dead (though George Melly's redoubtable mother, Maud, was still alive when he completed his). After all, the facts of childhood are not like historical dates, or the names of principal rivers, neutral things which can be recalled or not, depending on one's powers of memory. They are fraught with meaning, which will impose its own censorship if it had not been properly understood and digested.

My parents and I (their only child) have not had an easy relationship, but we can take some pride in having talked – argued – more than most families about the issues that have forced us apart. I do not think there are many other bones to be unearthed from their memory of my childhood; whatever lies buried now will remain undisturbed forever. We have probably gone as far as parents and adult children can in trying to elucidate the past from within the conflict of the prseent. Of course, I understood them better as parents once I became one myself, and I believe I know what motivated them, together and separately, to bring me up the way they did, but sadly this understanding did not help me retrieve my lost childhood. And so, while wanting to write about childhood, I found myself in the unhappy position of being cut off from the front and the rear, for I not only felt divorced from my childhood self, but I also felt that my own children were beginning to grow more mysterious and distant. Or, rather, they were mysterious and I was growing distant.

But then I had what seemed to me at the time a brilliant notion: I would cut through these knots with a single stroke by taking the children on a long summer trip in and around Wales, where I had lived as a boy and had been sent to school. In this way, I would be bringing my children face to face with my childhood and could expect to learn something new about both.

6

I was born in 1944 in Stackpole, a tiny village on the south coast of Dyfed, then Pembrokeshire, where my maternal grandfather farmed a thousand acres of beautiful countryside. Here we returned almost every Christmas and summer holiday. Meanwhile, I was brought up and first went to school in Liverpool, the city in which my father had also been brought up and was then practising as a solicitor. We lived close to the Otterspool promenade, and most of my early memories of Liverpool are associated with the River Mersey. At the age of eight I was sent to a boarding school in North Wales – Heronwater, near Abergele – which has since closed down. Later I was sent to Shrewsbury. Thus, my entire childhood was spent in Wales or on its borders. Yet, though I had a handful of very sharply etched memories concerning each of these places, I found it difficult to reconstruct the generality of my life in them. Since leaving Liverpool to work in London, I had hardly been back to any of these Welsh sites and scenes; furthermore, my parents left Liverpool themselves soon after to live near Chester, and so even visits to see them no longer involved going back 'home'. My plan was, therefore, to retrace some of the lineaments of my childhood by returning to its places, rather than its people, a journey that would take all of us into areas of unexplored territory.

In the event, I was unable to raise sufficient funds for our Grand Tour of Wales, and we had to content ourselves with a week's holiday in Stackpole. Its description occupies the whole entry under October in this book. I suppose it was predictable that my experiment would not yield the results for which I had hoped. After spending a week in one of the most significant and formative places of my life, introducing the children to my old haunts and watching them play as I had done at their age, I still did not feel I had come any closer to lifting the lid of childhood's mind. Nor did our holiday revive nearly as many forgotten incidents and experiences as I had anticipated.

Worse still, I had not used the opportunity to get closer to the children; the distance between us had, if anything, widened, and the fault was of course mine.

But, as this introduction is beginning to disclose, I was at that time emotionally very agitated and mentally very confused. I seemed to be drifting uncontrollably away from Sally, from the children and from our home; I seemed to be losing faith in the values of endurance and continuity which I had found so eloquently reflected in the trees and flowers of our local landscape, and which I had just celebrated in another book, now published – *The Living Landscape*. My preoccupation with a fugitive past, with the roots of my identity, was part of a fumbling attempt to soothe the turbulence and impose order on a situation that was, however, by then irretrievable. Events came to a climax in November. I hurt a great many people, and suddenly found that my marriage, my family and everything I had worked for, were crumbling. For the last ten years I had tried to think and live creatively, but somehow I had turned myself instead into a force of destruction.

Loyalty to Sally and unwillingness to write about the other person involved ensured that I would not discuss the difficulties that led to a crisis in our marriage. However, I decided I would write about my relationship with the children, insofar as it was possible to do so in isolation from our marriage, and try to account for my withdrawal from them. This book was originally conceived as a portrait of parenthood, among other things, and because I was certain I was by no means exceptional in finding that my feelings for my children were variable, I thought it important to describe the experience and dig up its origins. These days nothing is considered more odious than the failure properly to love one's children, but that only makes it all the harder for those whose parental feelings do waver to confess to it and live with them. In my case, even during periods of greatest alienation, my feelings for my children were never less than intense. My love for them never waned, but for long periods I was unable to attach my emotions securely to their object: my former love for them, which had been so fiercely committed, was left unfocused and unfulfilled. And so, in the hope that others might find it helpful, but much more in the hope that I could use the process as a therapy to help myself, I set out to trace the causes of my baneful confusion.

By then I had in fact begun this book, but it was easily adapted to my new, much more urgent purpose, for I discovered I had been unconsciously preparing the ground. (It is not difficult to read a sense of imminent catastrophe in my responses, recorded in October, to the menacing Stackpole landscape.) The book was planned to take the form of a journal, begun in September 1985, and divided into entries which were not dated, but were to be collected under months. I decided to keep that formula, and so the book as it now stands straddles the crisis of November, and runs from September 1985 to March 1986, when the winter of this tale was finally dispelled.

The entries comprise three strands of time, plaited into a single pigtail: the immediate present of writing, the period between 1977 and 1979 during which our two children were conceived and born, and the more distant past of my childhood. I have woven them together in an attempt to show how the past is always present in time being, especially when one is the parent of small children. Despite the drama surrounding some of the first-hand entries, the period of the second strand, which describes the impact of pregnancy and babies on our marriage, is the critical one. Parents are of course responsible in large measure for the formation of their children's characters, but it is not sufficiently recognized that the process is interactive, for one's character, as a parent, is to a significant degree made by one's children. For a great many people, nothing has a more decisive impact on their marriage than their first baby. This is especially so in these days when the interval between getting married and having children is growing longer, giving couples a chance to establish and enjoy a childless way of life, which in retrospect may seem an idyll of prosperity and freedom. It was not the case with us: in some ways that period of pregnancy and nappies was one of our happiest, but it certainly set in motion changes which took many years to complete, making them difficult to quantify and, on their destructive side, impossible to control. This book is the story of that unpredictable, occasionally explosive, evolution, which of course continues . . .

For the sake of clarity, I should mention that in 1977, when our daughter Tilly was born, we were living in Stowlangtoft, a small village near Bury St Edmunds in Suffolk, where we had moved two years earlier, leaving London and, in my case, a career in publishing. Our house, which we rented, was a large, ramshackle farmhouse, and it proved to be the most enjoyable house either of us had lived in as adults. It was also the most important house, for we held our wedding party there, I wrote three of my books there, and it was there we brought our son Jack home from hospital when he was born, in 1979, seventeen months after Tilly. (Our way of life in the derelict grandeur of this residence is the subject of *A Father's Diary*.) We continued to live in Stowlangtoft until the summer of 1984, when we moved to our present house, a rented cottage, which overlooks our old village, but stands by itself on the edge of a beautiful piece of woodland.

This book is the record of a marriage undergoing a crisis, but it is told from one side only. It could hardly be otherwise, unless it were a novel – but, alas, I am no novelist. Ever since we left London eleven years ago, Sally has supported my writing both morally and materially, never putting any obstacle in my way, even when it looked, as it did more than once, that my enterprise would never amount to more than penurious folly. Nor has she failed to support me this time, despite the fact that the book contains many episodes that are painful for her to see recalled, not least the moment when I threw her loyalty back in her face. Here is not the place for me to make apologies or ask for forgiveness; under the circumstances, to say anything here other than that I love her would be trivial.

The entries which refer to the running present were written on the spot, and in an effort to retain their authenticity I have hardly changed them since. If they appear ragged, disjointed, or even incoherent, I can only plead that they reflect my state of mind at the time.

Many people helped Sally and myself during the events of November, and I would like to express my gratitude to them. I feel a special debt to Sally's parents, to my friend Peter Fuller, and to Cath and John Catchpole, none of whom ever let us down, and I thank them too.

Finally, I want to say thank you with all my heart to Tilly and Jack; they will probably have to wait until they are parents themselves before they realize how much they have given me.

SEPTEMBER

September 1977 was the beginning for us, the month of Tilly's birth.

Sally's waters broke, according to the classic tradition, in the middle of the night, about three o'clock. I rang the hospital, mouthing the words, 'I think my wife has begun her contractions,' with a sense of overhearing a stranger and we were told to come in.

And so, under a star-filled sky, we bore off this huge fruit, which we had tended, protected and worried about as it had swollen and ripened through the summer. Now it was about to burst, and shed its kernel, and though we longed to release the new life inside, we feared for the tender, stretched skin that was so close to splitting. Sally was apprehensive, but not frightened. Her pregnancy had been trouble-free, our lives were relatively settled, and we ourselves felt ready to be parents. But, for all that, we were driving into the dark, in more senses than one. We felt like primitive heroes embarking on a mythic adventure into the unknown to be tested by the very gods of life and death themselves. We were so ill-equipped for our ordeal, having nothing to bring to the battle but Sally's courage, her naked body and the leaping life inside her, all of which seemed pitiful forces just then to wage against the great dark power that waited for her at the end of her journey.

Despite having done it a thousand times before, that journey was, we knew, the first of a completely new series: whatever was to happen in hospital, we would return utterly and irrecoverably changed. We were rushing towards a future that was unimaginable. Even though we had doted on other people's babies during the summer, finding the most tiresome, snotty-nosed creatures objects of profound interest, the person we were racing to give life to was an inconceivable stranger, who at that moment seemed far more formidable than a mere baby. Sally was in the grip of a black energy that would do anything, however destructive, to force its way out of her, into the night.

In the delivery suite, Sally was taken away for a bath and to be examined, while I was condemned, for a while, to the fate of all fathers before it was the convention for them to attend the birth of their babies. I was directed to the fathers' waiting room, a sordid hole, or so I thought it, though it was in fact an ordinary enough room, filled with chairs, stale magazines and the staler smell of cigarettes, to which I added in very full measure. Like a man acting out a cliché, I paced and smoked, smoked and paced. I would try to settle, but would think about Sally, and be on my feet again, lighting another cigarette. Because of the hour, only one low light burned, and for a while I was hardly aware of the other two men in the room. One was much younger than I, and he looked truly frightened. I tried to reassure him, but he asked if my wife was having her first baby and when I said yes, he turned his face away and stopped the conversation. He stared at the floor in horror, as if a life were about to be taken away, not given. After a while, he was led out to join his wife. I saw him later in the ward; he did not recognize me, and indeed I barely recognized him, for he was carrying his baby and was smiling ecstatically, as only newly made fathers do.

The other man lay in his service uniform across three chairs, and was sound asleep. At one point a nurse came in to tell him his wife had had a daughter. 'Not another fucking woman in the house,' he groaned, and went back to sleep.

It was during this grim interval that the uselessness of my role most depressed me. On our few visits to the hospital for check-ups, the staff had been unfailingly sympathetic to the father's presence and contribution, and everything we had read and been taught by our National Childbirth Trust teacher had encouraged us to believe in the value of the part I was to play. We had packed a flannel for me to wipe Sally's face, we had packed a book for me to read to her while I sat with her, and on the way to the hospital we had practised the song we had chosen to help her during the worst contractions ('Chatanooga Choo Choo'). But then, in that room, all these little strategems suddenly felt futile, empty devices to give me a role, which would in reality be quite marginal and dispensable, at least to the unstoppable physical process. I could never be more than an agitated but helpless observer; a hindrance, if anything. I could not bear the thought of Sally suffering, and I was very anxious about fainting or, worse, being sick. No doubt, an element of jealousy, or if not jealousy, of resentment over my unaccustomed impotence, sharpened my distress, but I had never felt so keenly on behalf of another as I did then.

Part of the trouble was that, as with so many other aspects of becoming a parent, I had no other memories or experiences to draw on for reassurance. We had been shown films of birth, and had found them very moving, but once we were inside hospital ourselves they no longer seemed applicable to the reality of what Sally was about to go through, and, for all I knew, was already going through. At that time I had no direct memory of anything being born, except – and this was not an encouraging precedent – a calf, which as a small boy on my grandfather's farm I had helped to deliver by holding a torch while the cowman hauled with all his strength on a rope attached to a pair of slimy legs protruding from what I took to be the cow's bottom.

Had Sally been keeping her sheep in those days, I think I would have felt slightly less anxious, and less redundant. During the last few springs, I have watched so many sheep giving birth that, in an emergency, which I am glad to say has not yet arisen, I believe I could deliver and keep alive a lamb by myself. Not that I would have felt any desire to deliver my own baby, but a greater familiarity with the literal flesh-and-blood mechanics of birth, and therefore a greater trust in the body's own natural resources, would have eased my agitation a little and spared me the feeling of being in the way. For, actually, everyone is in the way; or, rather, the husband is no more of an obstacle than the staff. However, I did not know that then, and I can only hope that when their turn comes my children, as prospective parents, will be able to derive some self-confidence from their memories of the many lambings they will have witnessed and assisted.

According to my notes, it was about four o'clock when I was summoned to join Sally in her room. She had taken a bath, was feeling fine and undergoing contractions every five minutes. I find it impossible to reconstruct the next few hours in any detail. I had intended to make a thorough record of the event as it unfolded, but this was a misconceived ambition. The few notes I did manage to make, during the many intervals when Sally was asleep between contractions, refer to the occurrence of her spasms, the injections and examinations she received, the comical and touching remarks she made under Pethidine ('I don't know whether I'm coming or going,' she woke to say at one point, looking very baffled), and the various calls I put through from the telephone outside her room. Sally's father was due to leave the country that very morning to take up a job in Nepal, and I rang him at seven to tell him Sally was in labour. Sadly, he had left for the airport before I could give him the final result. But, oddly enough, these factual notes revive next to no memories and coincide hardly at all with the memories I do have of that long morning, which are few but very vivid. I am sure some unconscious mechanism, stemming from biological necessity, is at work here, to ensure that the recollection of birth does not linger in the mind. Owing to the cumbersome size of our precocious skull, human birth is difficult, compared with that of other mammals, but the memory of the pain and fear involved must be wiped away, or at least softened, if a loving relationship with the baby is to begin at once without a sense of recrimination festering in the mother. And in the father, for that matter. Fortunately, in Sally's case, birth was not more than ordinarily painful, and if it was, this oblivion I am talking about has done a good job, for she too claims to remember only a few fragments of the whole episode.

After I joined Sally I made no notes for an hour or so. Of that period, I have very little memory, except of feeling closer to Sally than I had ever done before. All sense of redundancy was gone and forgotten. I also felt an almost uncontrollable excitement at the prospect of seeing our baby at last. We talked, but the pain was steadily worsening. Despite our breathing lessons and a half-hearted commitment to the idea of experiencing birth 'naturally', Sally put up no objection to the Pethidine when it was administered. This was done around six-fifteen, and within a quarter of an hour she became mildly delirious, complaining at first that 'it felt awful, but was lovely,' and then, after she had been asleep, that she had been away for a long time. During her contractions, which in fact came with unfailing regularity every four or five minutes, Sally would talk blearily, and I would rub her back, give her sips of water and hold her. Nurses came in occasionally, and I was always relieved to see them and hear their opinion of our progress, but the intimacy of those hours, which were mostly spent alone together, was very precious to me. I remember the voluptuous warmth of her body, as she lay on that clinical, ominously practical bed in that strange, half-dark room.

Because Sally was asleep for so much of the time, or at any rate beyond communication, some of the things I recall most sharply have nothing to do with her. Indeed, at one point, Sally herself said, during the lucid interval of a contraction, 'This must be a bit boring for you.' It wasn't, but I did have time on my hands, and as the night wore on I began to lose my grasp of how fast it was passing. The room was unbearably hot and we opened the windows. I got up every few minutes to stare down, mostly without seeing it, at the ornamental pond and its goldfish in the closed courtyard below. As the dawn came up, a pied wagtail appeared, strutting and bobbing on the strip of grass beside the pond. I also looked and looked, seeing everything, at Sally's swollen, turbulent body, wondering about her pain, wondering what would happen to her when the crisis finally came, and wondering who and what it was that was struggling to achieve life.

Later, we heard a woman in the next-door room screaming. A nurse put her head round the door and said she hoped Sally wasn't going to be a naughty girl like that. It was the only moment during the entire event when I felt angry. The screams continued, reaching horrific crescendos, but they did not seem to disconcert Sally. We agreed that the rooms should be sound-proofed, for, after all, if ever someone had the right to scream her head off, without worrying about the neighbours, it was then.

I recorded that at eight-twenty the Pethidine began to show signs of wearing off. The end was approaching and her contractions grew steadily more painful. For the first time since the injection, Sally became lucid and wanted to talk. Over the next three-quarters of an hour her contractions came to be gruelling and very sore. She reached the stage of wanting

20

to push, and I made my last note at nine minutes past nine, by which time both the houseman and the registrar had examined her. I remember thinking all three of us are about to be born – the baby, and Sally and I, as parents.

Thereafter, my memory loses all cogency. All I can recall is a turmoil of events, and an onslaught of feeling so chaotic, but intense, as to destroy the ability to make sense of what was happening to us. We were struggling with a force of nature, and also with each other. I felt as if I were in a street fight, not knowing whose side I was on. I hated watching the beating Sally was given, but found myself urging her to take still more pain: I made her push when she was tired and sore, and stopped her pushing when she was straining to do so. I desperately wanted to protect her, yet I was equally determined to force her through the ordeal needed to bring forth the baby. The staff encouraged me to shout instructions to her, which I did with all my strength, but without understanding what was expected of her, or what I was shouting. I bellowed in her ear, cajoled her, praised and drove her on. I held her hand during the worst contractions and only much later, when I came to dial the telephone, discovered that her clenching had badly bruised my fingers – hardly an injury to compare with Sally's suffering, but it hurt all the same!

The worst moment in this long brawl came towards the very end. Sally was given gas to ease the pain. She could not get the hang of using the mask. It smothered her. She pushed it back, crammed her head backwards and forwards, crying terribly. For the first time, her screaming became hysterical. The nurses tried to show her how to use it. I too pushed it on her face, but she just thrashed and yelled. Then, suddenly, she learnt the trick, and would not give up the mask. She was instantly addicted, shouting to have it back as it was torn away. The midwife got angry with her. I did not understand when she was supposed to use it, and when not. Again, I heard myself shouting meaningless, contradictory instructions over her screams.

It has become part of her personal mythology that Tilly was born at nine-thirty precisely; indeed, this fact was celebrated at school on her birthday, for she came back proudly announcing that 'Happy Birthday' had been sung in her honour at Assembly only six minutes after she had been born. It was not until I came to write this, eight years after, and looked up letters I had written then, that I realized whenever Sally or I tell her the story of her birthday, which she cannot hear too often, we always bring forward the moment of actual birth by more than an hour. Tilly was, in reality, born at ten-forty. Not only have Sally and I, between us, lost most memories of that morning, we have completely expunged from our account the hour that contained the grimmest parts.

One of the paradoxes – and privileges – of being a father is that you have a much clearer view of what is going on than the mother herself. I was able to tell Sally when the baby's head first appeared, bulging out for a second and then retreating as the contraction faded. I became hysterical, shouting again and again that the head showed, the head showed. And I shall never forget my first sight of that purple, bloody disc, with its matted wisp of black hair. Though I wanted to be at her head to comfort her and hold her hand, I could not resist running to the other end of the bed to stare at that ever-swelling bulge that was bursting, slowly bursting out of poor Sally's broken body.

Sally had recovered from her panic, and was now bearing down in earnest. I cried over her bravery. Only one more dreadful moment remained. It was decided that Sally should be cut to make way for the head, and I saw the midwife brandishing a kind of surgical secateur. I looked away, close to fainting for the first and only time, but could not avoid hearing the crunching, yielding sound of Sally's flesh as the scissors did their work. That horrific noise has stayed with me ever since.

After the cut had been made, events began to move very much faster. The staff behaved with a new urgency. A series of massive contractions folowed, during which Sally was urged to push with all her might. She did so, showing more courage than I had seen in anyone else, and certainly far more than I have myself. And suddenly, with a slithering dive into the breathing world, there was our baby, a purple, raging thing, its back arched, its legs bowed and feet bent up, its red body covered in mottled waxy stuff, and a thick cap of hair bloodily plastered to her mis-shaped head. For I knew she was a girl as she was being born. We had never much doubted we would have a girl, and, indeed, had not firmly fixed on any boy's name. 'It's a little girl, it's a little girl,' I repeated idiotically to Sally over and over, crying helplessly. The nurses inspected the baby for defects, but this was sheer pedantry; I could see at a glance that she was quite perfect and beautiful in every detail. I felt a great onrush of love, which had a force and immediacy I had never known before. Nor had I ever felt such pride and gratitude as I felt then for Sally. The baby was given to her, and we held her together, both crying.

Thus was Tilly born.

It is difficult to know how conscious the children are of the outside world, the world of our reality, which encloses them and determines the pattern of their lives. And it is still more difficult to know what impact it is making on them. What, for instance, does September mean to Tilly and Jack?

Living here in this beautiful spot, with a great panorama of farm land open to us on one side, and a dense wood of oak and ash screening our house on the other, Sally and I are very sensitive to the distinctive features of each month and season. Because of the sodden summer we have endured this year (1985), many of the sights and events we associate with

August have been delayed until now. The harvest has only recently been completed and most nights this week (mid-September) have been lit up by straw-burning in some corner of our expansive view. The bulk of the stubble has been burnt off in the usual way, in long swathes of flame, which from a distance gives the impression that the entire field has been set ablaze and is being consumed in the holocaust. But last night, as we drove home along the short lane that leads from Stowlangtoft to our wood, we were suddenly confronted with a different, and quite magical, spectacle. The straw in the field opposite the end of our lane had been gathered in huge, loose bundles, like dishevelled cones, and more than a hundred of these wild bonfires were burning merrily in the dark, which was so black we could not see the ground below them. They appeared to be floating, like a constellation of vast, unstable stars, in an upside-down sky.

Both the children were moved, as we were, but it was Tilly who gasped, 'How beautiful! I would like to sit near one all night.'

For us, September also means that every bush, hedge and clump of grass, the margins of the sugar beet field outside our house, the nettle beds that fill in the ragged edges of the wood, and even the shrubs in our scrappy garden are infested with young pheasants. A wet spring, followed by a wetter summer, has postponed their release into the woods, and they look less well developed than last year. Their feathers as yet barely cover their bodies, leaving their long, gawky legs looking ignominiously trouserless. When caught by surprise, they run cluelessly and headlong into the nearest cover, often trapping themselves in their haste. They fly with the greatest reluctance, and only for a few feet, rocketing upwards in a fluttering panic and then levelling into a low swooping glide. They much prefer to run, their heads held aloft, their bodies quite steady, and their legs appearing to revolve rather than stride, as if they were propelled by small pram wheels. These young birds are largely silent, too, and it will not be until the colder weather, when they will be big enough to shoot, that we will hear their harsh, but haunting 'kuttuc, kuttuc' noise of alarm echoing through the leafless trees and across the bare fields.

The wet weather has kept the wood itself greener than it would usually be at this time of year, but the leaves look stale with summer exhaustion and have not yet begun to turn colour or fall. The dog's mercury, however, which covers much of the open ground in the wood, is withering and going brown. Only a few wild flowers are to be seen. The rosebay willowherb are puffing out their feathered seeds; the odd straggling ragwort, whose other name is indeed 'summer farewell', still keeps its yellow flowers; and there is a small, somewhat furtive purple-blue flower in bloom, which to my annoyance I cannot identify, despite going through my book twice over.

This year the children have made more use of the wood, though they still dare not penetrate further than the immediate edge skirting our lane and garden. In their eyes, the wood is not an altogether happy feature of our new house. For the sake of the pheasants, one of the restrictions on our tenancy is that we should keep no pets, at least none capable of hunting. This prevents Jack from having a dog, for which he pines miserably, and Tilly from having a kitten (she does not want a cat!). They go into the wood mostly to make camps, but whether they have been aware of its changing character, month by month, during the summer, I cannot tell. I suspect not. It has been so wet this year we have only rarely been able to walk through it, and I have not shown them as many of its abundant wild flowers – my new passion – as I would have liked.

But if it is the case that, when left to rely on their own resources, they notice no more than the most unavoidable alterations in their landscape – snow, for example – this is not insensitivity on their part. They are both too young yet to have developed a sense of time which is able to assimilate the relatively slow flow of natural change. Their perception of the forward movement of time is still very limited. Certain events stand out like islands in the sea of the future – birthdays, Christmas, ends of term and so on – but they are only very vaguely placed on their chart of time, for their mere dates do not imply to them a precise location. They know that landfall will occur at some point on the voyage, and they look forward to that with keen anticipation, yet they are quite incapable of making calculations concerning distance over time. They see no further into the future than they look back into the past; both future and past close in on them like the horizon in a sea mist, and they happily concentrate on the small pool of sea in which they find themselves. In the same way, their sense of place is very confined. They exist in the here and now, inhering in it with an intensity that is never reproduced in adulthood, except at times of extreme suffering or elation. They literally do not see the wood for the trees. They make no comparisons, which is why their aesthetic taste tends to be negligible; they simply make use of whatever is given in their world, exploiting it as a facility for their games without considering its objective, independent reality. To this degree, they are artists: everything, regardless of its intrinsic significance, becomes material for their imaginative use.

The most salient event in September, for all of us, was of course the beginning of term, and a new academic year. The resumption of a very structured life was, I believe, welcome to the children, though they groaned over the prospect of returning to school. Patience, on both sides, was running low towards the end of the holidays, as the hordes of children who live round here wandered, like some nomadic tribe, from garden to garden, making their inevitable camps and leading an almost separate existence from their parents. We too fell into the nomadic mode, drifting from house to house to drink away the evenings before taking on the doomed struggle to get the children back to their own beds. Invariably, we would end up either childless, or in charge of a numberless, unidentifiable rubble of small, snoring bodies. Clothes, toys and other possessions, to say nothing of the children themselves, became hopelessly muddled up. When meals were not solitary affairs, they were major catering events, stripping the fridge bare in a single sitting. The children merged into a many-headed, collective being, one of whose heads might occasionally give me a fleeting 'Hi, Dad', though mostly this creature was only to be heard, at a distance, ullulating in the woods or at the far end of someone else's garden.

We parents marvelled at their capacity for sustained friendliness. Although there was the odd tiff, the occasional appeal for adult intervention, and some very rare requests to be taken home, the ebb and flow of their social life as a group was otherwise unbroken and harmonious. We also marvelled at the unfailing resourcefulness of their games: they were never at a loss for something to play, never called for more than the most rudimentary aids and materials, and hardly ever summoned adult help or inspiration. And yet, by the end of the holiday, I think they had begun to tire, not of each other, nor of their games, which were ever self-refreshing, but of their open-ended, free-wheeling way of life. They began to lose their bearings in relation to their families and their familiar structures of time and place. This was most noticeably expressed through the increasing friction we felt between the four of us on the few occasions when we did eat together as a family. We were continually telling them off for being rude, especially Tilly. But more than anything else her rudeness consisted in an indifference to our special status: we were just the staff attached to the house she happened to be eating in that night. Or so we felt, and we felt it very keenly.

At all events, despite their protests, they show every sign of settling cheerfully into the daily routine of going to school and returning to their own home afterwards. Things are still not right with Tilly, but then I have been aloof and preoccupied recently, which puts a far greater gap between us than their roving social life ever did.

There is nobody as unprepared for major responsibility and change as the parent-to-be who has had no previous experience of small children. At any rate, so it was in my case. Being an only child in a small family, and having no married cousins nearby, I had virtually no contact during my own childhood, adolescence and early adulthood with children younger than myself. The only memory I have of spending time with little children was during a summer holiday when I went to stay in Abersoch with a schoolfriend, whose elder sister and her family were also staying. I was about fifteen at the time, and brought to my games with my friend's nephews and nieces a hearty ineptitude, which embarrassed me and left them quite unamused, and sometimes even frightened. At one point I put the little girl on my shoulders and walked her around. This delighted her and, excited by my only success, I began to run; she was still more delighted, and so I ran faster and faster up and down the lawn, watched by her anxious mother. Inevitably, I tripped, and only sheer luck saved me from pitching her forward to crack her skull against the garden wall. I was abruptly relieved of my duties as an honorary uncle.

Apart from this unfortunate incident, I cannot recall ever having played with a small child, far less having handled a baby. Once Sally was pregnant, however, we both began to take an intense interest in every baby we came across. (Sally, I should add, comes from a much larger family than mine, and she not only had cousins with children, but friends too. Nonetheless, her concern for and curiosity about babies doubled when she became pregnant.) Babies had hitherto been a species for which I felt indifference, mixed with mild repugnance, insofar as I felt anything at all. Likewise, the preoccupations of their mothers had simply never crossed the threshold of my attention. But, suddenly, these creatures, and every aspect of their care, acquired a profound fascination: we stared and cooed into prams, we watched, spellbound, as nappies were changed, and we urgently discussed the relative merits of cots, beds and bassinets, a word I had never heard before. Indeed, we rapidly accumulated a whole new vocabulary and with airy expertise would bandy gynaecological and obstetric jargon, to the bafflement and boredom of our childless friends. I also became very priggish and doctrinaire on the subject of how parents should bring up their children, heaping especial disapproval on those whom I thought guilty of repressing their babies' natural expressiveness and curiosity. I swore I would never be that kind of parent.

However, in the event, none of this obsessional interest or abstract theorizing turned out to be of the slightest use in preparing us for the presence of an actual baby, our own baby. Perhaps here again a merciful function of the unconscious washes the memory clean, for it is only by resorting to my diary that I can go some way towards recapturing our feelings during those first few weeks after we brought Tilly home from hospital. So many of one's experiences arising out of the earliest months of being a parent seem to be effaced, and no one who is not in the very midst of caring for a baby, particularly a first baby, can truly appreciate both the turbulence and the claustrophobia which overwhelm the parents, or, rather, the mother. This naturally induced forgetfulness, if that is what it is, often prevents friends with older children from sympathizing, and in grandparents it may even allow a positive irritation to grow, as they see the looming shadows of overpossessiveness and mollycoddling. But, for the mother, being wholly submerged in the new baby's existence is an inescapable condition, from which there is no relief. At any rate, that is the way motherhood fell upon Sally. And I too, because I was at home throughout the day, felt myself irresistibly drawn into the vortex.

It goes without saying that Tilly was not merely the most beautiful baby in the ward, but the most beautiful ever born. (I remember some friends, whose baby was born well before ours, being annoyed by our cynical laughter when they reported that they had inspected all the other babies in their ward, and had come to the clear-sighted and wholly disinterested conclusion that their own was outstandingly the most handsome.) When I made my first visit to the hospital, following Tilly's birth, Sally was asleep and so I went to the crêche where the babies were parked in their transparent trolleys, wrapped in their blue and pink blankets. At the threshold, I was disconcerted to find a plastic name bracelet lying on the floor, which bore the words 'Baby Harrison'. I put it in my pocket and have kept it to this day; it has become an object of great veneration to its real owner, who often takes it out of my box of treasures to sigh sentimentally over its smallness. Despite the mild shock its discovery gave me, I located Tilly without hesitation, and only later thought of checking that her bracelet was in fact missing. It was. Apart from her conspicuous looks, she was distinguishable by being the hairiest baby in the crêche. When her immense shock of black hair was first washed and dried, a service performed by a nurse for the education of the other mothers whose bald offspring no doubt acquired their hair in time, it rose from the top of her head in a sable nimbus, like a piece of exotic plumage.

Tilly was a small baby, weighing in at 5 lbs 9 oz, but to us she seemed tiny, a fragile miniature. Freshly wrapped and carried in a basket, she was brought home like a parcel, an item of shopping, a precious new possession we had just obtained in town. However, in spite of her midget size, she immediately invaded the entire house, from attic to cellar. Not that we resented her occupation, but we were ceaselessly conscious of her presence, which seemed to throb in every corner with its own all-pervasive energy, even when she was asleep. From the moment we carried her through the door, our lives, all our physical and mental energies, were monopolized by the diminutive being we had created.

Children, no matter how knowing or manipulative, never again exercise as much power as they do when they are new-born babies. Though innocent, babies are tyrannical. Their calls must be answered, their demands met, their needs fulfilled and anticipated. A baby's cry cannot be ignored; at any rate, we could not ignore Tilly's crying. It aroused in us some very primitive instinct, which would not be denied and produced acute anxiety until we took action. The softest whimper, unheard by most, and insignificant to other parents, rang in our heads like a fire bell. Our days and nights were concentrated into a continual emergency, broken by rare interludes of deep contentment when Tilly had been satisfactorily fed and had fallen asleep. Mostly, however, our state of mind was one of barely controlled panic. Without ever putting it explicitly into words, we knew that we were engaged in a life or death struggle, for as first-time parents we had no understanding of the fierce and tenacious grasp babies have on existence.

Over the last fortnight, the news has been dominated by a series of gruesome cases of child abuse, which have demonstrated, all too graphically, that it requires maltreatment on a truly barbaric scale actually to kill a child. Also, news keeps coming in of babies being found in the rubble of Mexico City's maternity hospital. So far, they have been rescued seven days after the earthquake first struck, and the hospital staff are advising that it will be worth continuing to search for yet another five days. The most extraordinary aspect of these discoveries is that, far from being damaged by their deprivation of food and water, the majority of the babies are emerging from their sepulchres in a state of near perfect health.

We were only conscious, however, of the amateurish inadequacy of our efforts, which we saw as being all that stood between our frail new life and extinction. I was convinced too that the slightest discomfort or frustration would score a deep and everlasting mark in Tilly's personality. She was, I believed, not only wholly dependent on us for her physical survival, in itself a novel and terrifying experience, but also for the happy and healthy fulfilment of her mental being. To leave her crying for one minute longer than necessary was to run the risk of permanently deforming her character.

All this now seems as incredible as it was absurd, particularly when I compare it with our treatment of the new-born Jack seventeen months later, which was sometimes casual to the point of neglect. But, at the time, we knew no better, and would not let anyone tell us.

Tilly's birthday party usually signals the end of summer, being the last big children's event to take place out of doors. But this year's, her eighth, heralds the beginning of autumn, for our fraud of a summer gave up the pretence on the first of September and it is now continuously cold.

Their parties usually have a theme. Two years ago the weather was hot enough for her to throw a Dallas-style poolside party, and the effect of glamorous high-living was not at all spoilt by the fact that the guests in their chic bikinis lolled round a plastic paddling pool no bigger than a bath. This time she chose to have a disco party, currently the fashionable thing among the eight-year-old crowd. Because of the weather, it had to be held inside somewhere, so Sally cleared and decorated the little barn next to our house, while I, with many misgivings, installed my precious record player. Our friend, the Admiral, donated some old ship's signal flags for the occasion, and I nailed them round the barn door, where they flapped gaily in the chill breeze. Everything looked quite splendid by six o'clock, when the guests began to gather, all dressed and made up for dancing. We put on the first record and left them to it.

Ten minutes later, I listened out for sounds of revelry, but could hear nothing. I went over to the barn and discovered a knot of little girls shivering in the half-dark, too cold to dance, too shy to come and say so. I dragged across our mobile gas fire, only to find that it had run out of gas. However, by the time I returned from my mercy dash to the garage to buy a new bottle, the dancing was under way and when I switched on the fire I was told to turn it off straightaway by a flushed and panting Tilly.

This year's party was made exceptional by the inclusion of an entertainment spot in the shape of a circus, which Tilly and three of her friends had previously prepared and rehearsed. Though the production had originally been supervised by Sally, and later adapted to incorporate Jack, all the ideas were their own. This was a circus in the grand style of The Greatest Show On Earth. Among its many featured acts, as described in their announcements, were The Most Wonderful Ballet Dancer In The World (poignantly writhing in complete silence), The Most Funniest Clown In The World (Jack!), The Most Famous Gymnastic and The Black Panther (Tilly, terrifying in her cat suit, under the command of a whip-cracking trainer). Our unfortunate jerbil, having played its part in the magician's act by vanishing from a hat, while the audience was

33

made to close its eyes, was required to appear with the rest of the cast in the line-up for The Grand Finale. As they took their bow, Tilly held it aloft in a fierce grip, partly to make sure it did not escape, and partly to show that it too was bowing.

For once, the acts were not allowed to drag on interminably, giving pleasure to no one but the insatiably self-regarding performer. A low whistle from the wings, which, if not responded to immediately, was followed by a louder, more insistent one, brought each piece to an end well within the patience of even the adult part of the audience. And there were some notably inventive touches. At one point, a little girl was shown standing in a cupboard, the door was then shut, her legs were sawn off, and the door opened again to reveal her apparently legless torso suspended in mid-air. The performers ranged in age from eight to three, and although the older ones had thought up most of the material, none was without a vigorous sense of theatre. The whole show, not excepting Jack's shamelessly low clowning, was very well received by its all-girl audience.

After the circus, Tilly cut her cake. In deference to her present obsession with horses, Sally had designed it to look like a riding school: a square of sponge iced brown to represent mud and decorated with toy horses, fences, trees and grooms. 'Happy Birthday' was sung, accompanied by Jack on the family bugle, which Sally's Dad had brought with him. Then, at last, the girls got down to serious dancing, leaving the adults to get down to some serious drinking in the kitchen, confident that they would not be required for another hour. Jack, and the lone male friend he had been permitted, also retired to build Leggo space rockets.

It was an altogether memorable evening. At the end I found myself hoping it would not be the last of such parties Tilly would hold. Among the guests had been a couple of older friends from school, sophisticates of nine, who, though they had responded to the circus, had been ostentatiously bored by the treasure hunt and other games, and had stood wearily watching the little ones, their hands on their hips, their lip-sticked mouths turned down in disdain. I know one has to let children grow up at more or less their own pace, but I felt sorry that these girls had been cut off from the infantile playfulness and had learnt so early that it was not befitting their dignity to indulge in childish things.

Around this time, in the September of Jack's first year (1979), seven months after he had been born, another kind of birth took place. It was silent, unmarked, unnoticed by anyone else and quite painless. This was the birth of my love for Jack. Like an unborn creature, it had been alive and steadily growing, but not until that September did it finally emerge as a fully developed being. Before then I had not rejected him, or felt cool towards him, or indeed felt any lack of love for him, but I had felt awkward with him, embarrassed even, as if he were a strange species or a foreigner whose ways I did not under-stand. In a word, I did not know how to express my affection for him. With Tilly it had been altogether different: with her I had felt an instantaneous rapport and I had instinctively known how to handle and treat her. But with Jack it took those seven months to achieve the same carefree, unthinking, jolly exchange of love I had enjoyed with Tilly from the start.

I think the explanation for this feeling of estrangement from my own son is simple enough, though the experience of it was not at all simple to undergo. No matter how imaginative one's interpretation of a baby's verbal and facial signals, the fact is that the chief medium of communication with a baby is touch. But as a man, at any rate as a middle-class Englishman of my age, one is entirely unused to exchanging physical affection with other men. As men go, I believe I probably give my affection more easily than most, and am more willing to be open about my feelings. Furthermore, I find it is men, rather than women, apart from Sally, in whom I confide. However, my friendships with men involve next to no direct physical contact. I occasionally put my arm round someone's shoulders, or squeeze his arm, but only at moments of emotional intensity, when I feel the other person needs exceptional reassurance. It is very rare for me to give, or receive, a spontaneous touch of casual friendliness, except the formal handshake. And even when I do make such a gesture, I am always aware that it is strictly controlled by a very rigid convention, whose limits are quickly reached and nervously maintained on both sides. The gesture itself is invariably abrupt, brief and intended to convey far more than it dares express overtly. Perhaps I have always been rather frigid about what might be called social touching, but from the few women whom I do hug or kiss in friendliness there is an immediately warm response, a yielding closeness that is a playful mockery of receiving a sexual advance, whereas from men there is a careful resistance, which matches my own equally careful restraint. I do not regret any of this; I merely note it as a curiosity of our social relations.

The only man with whom I have shared a physically expressed affection is of course my father. When I was a small boy, he always held my hand on walks and sat me in his lap to watch television. I have a vivid memory, which I cannot date, of sprawling on his knee and feeling I was too big and old to do so, but also feeling that I did not want to get off. He was most sociable in the bath and would regale me in his tuneless voice, which I much admired, with his repertoire of ballads and cowboy songs. 'Cool Water' was one of my favourites and I have never heard it sung since, even by Frankie Lane, with the thrilling note of drama my father, and the acoustics of our bathroom, used to give to it. I got tremendous enjoyment too from the histrionic wrestling matches we used to have together after Sunday lunch – what they did to the poor man's digestion, I cannot think – when we would roll and struggle on the carpet and he would let me inflict agonizing defeat on him. Obviously, these games stopped as I grew older and bigger, and I suppose I reached the stage when I would have been embarrassed by his touching me. When we meet now, we do not kiss, we shake hands.

In his dealings with adults, my father, with whom after all I share the same middle-class background, is as restrained as I am about social touching, and so I am grateful to him for his unstinted physical affection. Children unquestionably thrive on it, and no child was ever toughened up or prepared for the rigours of life by being deprived of it, though I have heard that theory preached by more than one father in our circle of acquaintances, and in relation to girls as well as boys. A Victorian tradition of masculinity continues to have an influence: keeping your feelings masked and under restraint is still a condition of manhood, which is translated into repressive ideas about the upbringing of boys and the amount of affection (hugging and kissing) appropriate to their future effectiveness as men. I am sure this is damaging. A child who has been loved across the whole range of emotional expression stands at least a reasonable chance of making and receiving emotional advances when his or her time comes in adulthood. Although my own relationships with women have not always been successful, and have occasionally been disastrous, I have managed to keep my belief in the possibility of a good relationship because built into me was this bedrock of assurance that physical, and thus sexual affection could be successfully exchanged.

When Tilly was born her body seemed to me a delightful thing, to be played with, caressed, tickled and given every kind of loving, stimulating attention. But, despite the seventeen months of practice I had enjoyed with Tilly, when Jack was born I found it difficult to relate to his body, which seemed to confront me as a powerful, threatening force, keeping me at bay. I was shy with him (how absurd this sounds as I write it now) and rather formal in my handling of him, even though I was changing, feeding and looking after him every day. I had felt the same tumultuous onrush of love for him when he was born as I had felt for Tilly, and yet I was embarrassed to indulge in the idiotic, joky endearments which were such a happy feature of my relationship with Tilly. I should not exaggerate any of this; I am only talking about shades of difference. Yet I was conscious of the difference, slight as it was, which was one of quality, as well as degree. In time, as I said, I established an equally relaxed playfulness with Jack, though it has always remained different in style from that with Tilly, as it was bound to do. Nonetheless, it took those seven months before I was able to write in my diary that Jack is 'no longer a stranger here'.

Since she had already had her party, I feared Tilly's actual birthday would fall rather flat, but in the event she seemed excited and pleased by everything that happened. Quicker than Jack, she has learnt to adapt her expectations to reality as it changes – something her father has never learnt, and never will.

Jack turned out to be the first to wake this morning – another sign of her maturity – and he came tottering into our bedroom very early to ask where her presents had been hidden. I showed him and sent him back to bed, but he was soon downstairs again, announcing that Tilly was now awake and ready to receive her gifts. We took them upstairs and found her lying beside Sally in our bed, propped up on the pillows in her usual queenly style. Because of the party, her parcels only amounted to a small pile, but she did not appear to be dismayed. She did, however, make the opening ceremony last as long as possible by lingering over each card, studying its picture, cooing over its message, and carefully putting it back in its envelope, before turning to her parcels, over which she loitered still more. This struck me as an impressively positive way of dealing with what probably was a disappointment, for in the past she had ripped open her presents, hardly looking at them in her hurry to get at the next one, strewing paper and cards everywhere.

We gave her a pair of shoes – sling-backs, as requested, for they are the height of chic in Class 3. We had bought an official present for Jack to give her, but he insisted on organizing another of his own. He had found a long-lost brooch of hers, which he wrapped in layers of tissue paper and bound up in an impenetrable case of Selotape. This she received as graciously as her other presents.

Finally, we took her downstairs to the kitchen to see her new bike. She had more or less known that her 'big present' was to be a bike, and had only stipulated that it should have 'shiny paint'. In fact, being second-hand and well-used, its paintwork was far from shiny, but because it was an adult bike of exactly the same make as Cath's (the mother of her great friend, Ruth), she was nonetheless delighted with it. Although we had screwed down its handlebars and saddle to their lowest point, we were still worried that it would be too big for her. However, once aboard, she rode it like a hunter.

When they returned from school this afternoon, Sally and I were painting the kitchen (a job that has taken us a mere twelve months to get round to doing). Jack disappeared to his camp in the woods, but Tilly stayed behind to help us. As a rule, 'helping' with painting is something to be dreaded and curtailed. Yet, on this occasion, Tilly not only painted an entire window ledge with skill and concentration, but also displayed a cool, poised manner neither of us had witnessed before.

'How's your bit going, Dad?' she asked me, as I worked beside her on the window frame.

'All right. How's yours going?'

'I think it will be satisfactory,' she replied, with quite unconscious aplomb.

It is true that her new eight-year-old self soon collapsed back into her familiar, younger self, as she stamped her foot and petulantly clamoured for something that had been absolutely prohibited, but there was no question that for half an hour or so a new high-water mark of maturity had been registered.

These moments induce very mixed feelings. Children must grow up and parents must encourage and congratulate, but my pride is always tinged with a melancholy awareness that each of these little steps on the way to maturity is a step away from us. In some ways, of course, their moves towards independence are welcome and bring relief, yet they still hint at the separation to come, which I foresee as an emptiness. I look back on our family life of only three or four years ago, and can hardly recognize the degree to which we were all so tightly locked together. At times, it seemed we were all sewn into the same small suit, all struggling and writhing to make each other comfortable and win some comfort for ourselves. That terrible sense of constriction has gone, not least because the children are now both at school, but with it has also gone that joyous feeling of complete mutuality, which the presence of small children can create within a family.

Occasionally, when they have lost or broken something, or

some other tragedy has struck, I see despair in my children's faces, that true despair which comes from realizing they are face to face with an unappealable absolute and the toy is lost forever or unmendable. In these matters, their grasp of the practicable is, fortunately, very unsound and a touch of glue or an astute search will soon restore their peace of mind. And, when a happy outcome is not possible, we comfort them with what are, essentially, lies, attempting to make the truth tolerable, or simply diverting their attention to pleasanter things. But, for that moment, their despair is authentic, with all hope dead and consolation out of the question, or so it was for me at their age.

Later in life, you again realize there are certain absolutes which will yield no permanent comfort or release, and then your old childhood sense of hopelessness is revived with all its original intensity, but this time on a chronic basis. You are driven to acknowledge that there are ambitions which will never be fulfilled, no matter how hard you strain; frustrations which will never be appeased, but will itch and infuriate to the day of your death; regrets which will never cease to sting; griefs which cannot be cried away; and that you will die still raging for satisfactions which have eluded you all your life.

Perhaps old age brings its own respite. I hope so, though for myself I do not relish the prospect of longevity, nor do I look forward to putting the doubtful privileges of age to the test. The struggle to squeeze the most from one's limited talents, and keep at bay the wolves of depression, is hard enough even in one's alleged prime. The idea, therefore, of continuing to wage this struggle with declining powers, with increased dependence on others, and in failing health, seems to offer nothing except a new circle of despair. I would not go to my grave with too many regrets if I were to be cut down in midfight, still fighting and failing, but at least not sunk in impotent decay.

At the moment, however, I feel as if I am in limbo, waiting for something, though I don't know what. I only know I am in a state of insupportable impatience, from which I can get no relief. I am continually agitated from within, while the world outside does nothing but irritate me. When I am not unpleasant to Sally, I am cold; this house, this beautiful cottage, which has been the envy of our friends over the summer, closes on me like a prison cell; I ignore the children, who ask so little of me and give so much, and when I do notice them, it is only to feel either angry or guilty. I am smoking lethal quantities of cigarettes; I drink too early in the day and too late at night. And the worst of it is, I can't find the cause. I can think of a dozen things that might have unsettled me, but none of them seems sufficient to provoke the fiendish energy that drives my restlessness. This is a very dangerous mood, and I hope it is dispelled by our trip to Pembrokeshire.

OCTOBER

On the final leg of our holiday journey we followed the signs to Stackpole, then to Stackpole Quay itself, and found ourselves on a winding road overlooking the sea, and there, for the first time, spread out below and before us, lay a typical stretch of Pembrokeshire coastline. Curving far away from us, in the shape of a battered sickle, was an erratic line of bays and headlands, coves and points, each one bitten out of its sheer grey or red cliffs by a sea that was then an innocuous emerald, except where it licked a white, dangerous spume from the feet of the rocks.

Sadly, this was the moment at which Jack's high spirits finally broke. Since approaching Pembroke, we had been trying to impress on them the fact that we were now travelling through the country of Daddy's childhood holidays. Tilly had responded with empty, though correct, politeness, but Jack had opted for a more perverse reaction, partly as a residue of their generally hilarious mood, and partly in resistance to our admittedly heavy-handed propaganda. 'It's 'orrible,' he said to everything we pointed out, hoping to elicit giggles from Tilly. He even refused to acknowledge the splendour of Pembroke Castle, although I could tell he was secretly awed by its huge keep and sprawling curtain wall, compared with which our Suffolk castles are no more than toy forts. Sally became cross with him when we finally sighted the coast, for the view was truly spectacular and quite unlike anything he, or she, for that matter, had ever seen before. And so, just as we were about to turn a corner and drop down the quay, he collapsed into tears, wailing that everyone was being 'orrible to him. We attempted to soothe him, we threatened him, we ground our teeth in silent rage, and in the end I simply drove on. It had been a very long journey.

My instinct was correct. The excitement of unpacking the car and moving into a new house, especially one so close to the sea, was enough to revive him instantly. We parked, collected our key and carried a couple of suitcases to the door, but the sound of the waves was irresistible. We walked across a little patch of meadow, the children running ahead, and were suddenly confronted by the sea – not an expanse of colour washing the horizon, glimpsed through breaks in the hedge from a car window, but the real, living sea, lashing and foaming over the stones at our feet. The tide was low and the children made immediately for the sea's edge, slithering over the wet rocks and, deaf to our instructions, soaking their shoes in the idle waves. Like most small coves along the coast, this one is clogged with a rubble of sea-smoothed boulders scattered on a gravel of tiny pebbles and chips. The rock that forms its pitted floor and crumbling walls is grey and black, except where lichen has managed to paint yellow streaks on outcrops beyond the reach of the tide, but the shingle is made up of all the colours of the sea, dark greens, slate blues and streaks of white running like foam across the backs and through the bones of the greyest stones.

Standing in the middle of the cove and marking its original edge is a large knoll of rock, the size and shape of a derelict cottage. Once a part of the cliff, it is now a discarded flake of the mainland, which the tide turns into an island. Showing an alarming ignorance of the dangers held by these fragile edifices, Tilly was soon scaling the rock and dancing on its treacherous, grassy roof, which on its sea front presented a clean drop into the water. We all joined her and peered down the precipice. I felt that strange melting sensation in the groin that fear of height induces, and found Jack clinging anxiously to my trouser leg, begging us to go down. Back on the shingle, we left the children to explore the rock pools and collect pebbles.

Much to my surprise, I had experienced an intense response to this cove, for it is not especially dramatic by Pembrokeshire standards, and was not one of the landmarks of my childhood; indeed, I had confused it with the cove next door, which in fact contains the quay lending its name to the farm where we were staying. No, I did not respond to any memory of the place, nor to the character of its rocks, but to the action of the sea itself. Although the tide was out, the weather calm and the evening soft and balmy, the mere sight of the water's restless, uneasy motion accorded exactly with the submerged agitation stirring the depths of my mind. I watched a lethargic wave sidling round the rocks, just rippling the casual swell. Without warning, it struck a terrible blow, detonating massive charges of spray and shaking the whole cove, and I recognized my own unappeasable turmoil. It too was concealed beneath a tranquil surface, hiding its potential for sudden fury and wanton breakage. I know that over the last few weeks my mood has undergone its own equinox, and my emotional tides have run higher than usual, but my response to the sea's action was no temporary affinity; I saw in it the expression of some elemental, permanent part of myself, which neither the Suffolk landscape nor the Norfolk coastline had ever expressed.

The flat expanses of estuary mud and shimmering water, which we see every year on our holidays in Burnham Overy Staithe on the north Norfolk coast, possess their own beauty – and menace – which no one has captured more disturbingly than George Crabbe in his Aldeburgh poems. I have come to identify with those eerie meltings of mud, water and sky which slide seamlessly towards a distant emptiness, curtailed not by horizons, but the failing of sight. I have seen in them something of my own lack of definable shape; I have seen in that limitless dissolving of land and sea into light the vagueness of my identity, my known self. But, being here in Pembrokeshire for the first time in many years, and having childhood so much on my mind, I suddenly felt that this coastline, with its savage sea and tormented cliffs, was not merely the place of my birth, but had been an active instrument in the making of my character.

In 1938, my maternal grandfather, John E. Bennion, resigned from a secure job to take the tenancy of the Home Farm, Stackpole, which was then owned by the Earl of Cawdor. He was aged forty-nine. The advertisement in *The Field*, which had originally tempted him to make this radical change in his life, described the holding as 'A Famous Home Farm to let in South Pembrokeshire (Little England beyond Wales) . . . 554 acres, 416 of parks and pastures (all well watered) and 158 acres of rich tillage and clover leys: extra fine and roomy buildings, and very nice house, four miles south of Pembroke; situated amongst charming scenery and near bathing beaches, lakes and beauty spots; very mild and temperate climate . . .' While the advertisement flattered the house, which was never 'nice', even after my grandmother's extensive renovations, it modestly understated the beauty of Stackpole's situation, and did no justice to the unique character of its coastline.

Here is not the place to tell the story of my grandfather's middle-aged adventure, which in any case he has told himself in his posthumously published autobiography, *Stackpole and the Bennions*. It is enough to say that he made a great success of his second career, becoming something of a legend in his adopted county and among his new farming colleagues. Nor, as I have been discovering this week, has his name been forgotten yet, more than twenty years after his death. As a farmer, he was certainly a remarkable man; as a grandfather, however, he was . . . If I could complete that sentence without hesitating, I would probably not have felt the same urge to revisit the scenes of his triumph and my childhood; for, whatever else this trip into the past may be, it is not an exercise in nostalgia.

The farm, my grandparents, and my uncle's family, who lived nearby, played a central part in the life of my family throughout my childhood. Every Christmas and summer we used to travel down from Liverpool, where my father worked as a solicitor, to spend our holidays. Indeed we were staying there for Christmas when my grandfather died. After his death, the farm went through a series of complicated sales and partitions: the house is still occupied by a farmer, who is responsible for some of the land, but most of those 'extra fine and roomy buildings', which was a fair description, have been bought by the National Trust, along with the lakes below the farm, the lovely woods which surround them and the coastline itself.

In my grandfather's day, pigs were kept on a separate little farm unit, a mile or so away from the Home Farm. It was known as Quay Farm, because it was located at the very edge of the sea, beside a pair of small coves, one of which had been equipped with a quay built of limestone blocks. Evidently, this facility had been installed in the nineteenth century for the private use of the Cawdor mansion, whose coal supplies were unloaded there in order to save the expense of having them hauled overland. Of the farm in its pig era, I have very few memories, though I must have been taken there many times. In fact, I recall only two things with any clarity: the deep-throated sound of pigs gorging themselves on acorns in the woods above the farm, and a pair of fascinatingly rigid leather shorts habitually worn by the stockman in all weathers. At all events, the farmhouse and its buildings have now been converted by the National Trust into holiday accommodation, and these new cottages have been named in commemoration of their agricultural past: Farm, Byre, Dairy and Granary cottage.

It was to Granary cottage that I brought my family on this holiday. By a suitable irony, it was the very building that used to house the pigs. Such was my return to the grandeurs of my childhood.

I was born in October, on the twenty-third, and partly for this egotistical reason it has always been my favourite month, and autumn my favourite season. Just as the children are fascinated by the story of their birth, which has acquired legendary status in their eyes, I enjoy the fact that the conditions under which I was born have their touch of melodrama. I suppose we all like to think that the occasion of our arrival does not go unnoticed by the gods and is marked by some salute from nature or some freak of circumstance. When Sally and I first brought Tilly home from hospital we stood at the back door of the farm where we then lived and, in the absurd way of new parents, we held her up to admire the orange harvest moon which happened to be hanging like a hot air balloon just above the pig sheds opposite. As we did so, we heard the faint strains of 'Waltzing Matilda' being sung at the farm's harvest supper in a barn across the yard. Nobody at the supper could have known that we were standing there at that moment, nor even that we had chosen Matilda as a name, and so this little coincidence seemed to carry the deepest significance: it was a gift to our new-born child, a small, but unmistakable gesture of welcome.

My birth was not attended by Shakespearean portents, but nature did conspire to dramatize it, at least in the minds of those immediately involved. My mother was living with her parents on their farm in Stackpole on the south Pembrokeshire coast, and my father, who had recently been invalided out of the army and was awaiting the results of his solicitor's finals, was able to join her before the predicted date of her labour. In the event, my unborn self delayed for more than a fortnight, a piece of behaviour which only goes to show what little importance should be attached to such things, for my adult character is marked by both impatience and officious punctuality. However, during the interval, the October gales had begun to blow. These are notoriously ferocious on that part of the coast, and in 1944 they raged with exceptional violence. My mother was determined to have her baby at home, but because the family doctor lived a few miles away, in Pembroke Dock, it was feared that when her labour finally started the telephone line might be down, or, worse, the farm itself might be cut off by flooding and deprived of electricity. My grandmother therefore arranged to have half a dozen large milk churns filled each day with fresh water and kept in readiness just outside the house. She also prepared a battery of oil lamps, their wicks trimmed and tanks filled.

The rains fell, the winds roared, the highest tides of the year smashed against Broadhaven's cliffs a mile away, and the household waited. But when at last my mother's own waters broke around midnight, the midwife was able to bicycle from Stackpole village without difficulty, and my mother, except for being terrified by seeing straps tied to the bedhead for her to grasp in her forthcoming agony, bore her baby without more than ordinary difficulty. The doctor arrived in the early hours, delivered me with forceps and pronounced me fit and intact. My father, as was the custom then, spent the night apart, sleeping on a sofa in the sitting room, and had to be woken at eight o'clock to be told he had a son. The first sounds I heard, as I lay beside my mother in the daylight, must have been those of the farmyard below starting its day's work: cows plodding with staid urgency through their own mire towards the milking parlour, tractors warming up their engines, and my grandfather, always at his most genial before breakfast, bustling among his men.

Despite the momentous weather, no birth could have been more straightforward. The churns were emptied and returned to the dairy, the lamps put away until the next emergency. And yet, I still like to think of myself as a child of the storm, to think that something of my own inner turbulence derives, not just from ordinary neurosis, but from that wild equinox which witnessed my birth.

At the first opportunity, I took Sally and the children to see Home Farm, but our visit merely confused the children. The whole complex was originally built so that the house, barns and shed formed a rectangle, enclosing a classic farmyard. But now the yard has been divided by a low, curved wall, which segregates the house from the rest, and some of the buildings have been converted by the National Trust into workshops and offices. Apart from a bewildered, defensive collie barking near the house, there was no sign of anything the children associated with farming. It was disconcerting to see the old yard so transformed, because this was the chief arena of my grandfather's energy. Yet, since the place was no longer viable as a farm, it was heartening at least to find another kind of energy in action, which was providing amusement and education. The old dairy rang with the voices of schoolchildren as they gathered around a small fleet of minibuses to go on a field trip to the coast; one of the buses, looking like a strange upside-down craft, was loaded with canoes, and another was specially equipped to accommodate disabled children.

More distressing to me, however, was the sight of the barn and cow sheds, which have been allowed to fall into decay and are now being demolished to make way for a swimming pool and other facilities for the disabled. The front end of the barn, which forms part of the yard's quadrangle, still stands intact, the arms of the Cawdors displayed in a design of coloured stone above its gaping doors. But the grain stores and other buildings behind it, all built out of the local grey limestone which makes the farm buildings in the area so handsome, have collapsed in ruins. At the far end is a watch tower, which once used to house a bell, and where, so I remember being told as a child, my grandfather kept guard during the war, his rifle at the ready, waiting to repel the invading Germans.

In fact, by a strange irony, the enemy did take up occupation, for as the war went on the farm was given prisoners-of-war to work on the land, and the barn below the tower was turned into a prison block. I believe they were mostly Italians, though Germans were also sent to the farm from a nearby camp. A few of them stayed behind after the war to marry local girls, and I can remember Carl, a gifted carpenter, who was always friendly to me, as well as Hans, the groom, who was given the thankless task of teaching me to ride. He addressed me as 'Frizzer'.

'Grip ze knees, Frizzer,' he would shout at me, as the pony ambled in weary circles, keeping a wistful eye on its stable. The creature had never been known to break into a trot, far less a canter, and was safer to ride than an armchair, but I never learnt to do anything except hug its neck in a terrified, bouncing stranglehold.

I believe the stables, where these ignominious lessons took place, are still in use, but the roofs and walls surrounding the watch tower have caved in, leaving it to stagger for a while in solitary dilapidation. We stared up at it gloomily, for although in reality it was never used by my grandfather, or anyone else, it seemed to symbolize the decline and fall of his small empire. Like a stack rock, it has become detached from its original structure and is riddled with holes in its foundations, which will soon bring it down; in the meanwhile, the grass growing among its smashed slates serves the birds as a nesting place.

Adjacent to the barn was a quadrangle of shippons, which had been filled in with other sheds to form a sort of cattle village, incorporating a milking parlour, a maternity ward, calf pens, and a mightily reinforced chamber to house the resident bull, whose woolly forehead my grandfather would always scratch as he made his daily inspection of the stock. I once tried to imitate him and was punished with a bruised finger, which the bull neatly crushed into the wall with its horn. These cow sheds were nonetheless one of my favourite haunts. I would retire here when the men had gone home for their lunch and let the calves suck my hands with their Velcro tongues, or bounce the little nuggets of cattle cake, which had been weighed to the ounce in buckets, around the corrugated iron roofs.

Livestock was the pride of the farm. The low beams of the oldest buildings were thickly festooned with rosettes awarded in shows all over the country. If my grandfather had genius, it was probably for breeding Friesians, and he achieved the distinction, which I am told has yet to be rivalled, of having a cow, grandly named Stackpole Sham Marthema, win the Supreme Championship at the Royal Dairy Show a few weeks before winning another Championship at Smithfield with a bullock. The first of these victories took place on his seventy-third birthday, and he was dead shortly after the second.

Before a show, these magnificent animals would be taken into the yard, tethered to a wall, and prepared for their appearance like beauty queens. They were washed, shampooed, washed again, dried, powdered, brushed and decorated. Then they were led into the cattle box to be driven to the showground, where the whole procedure was repeated. Now, however, both the beasts and their buildings have gone; the old shippons are nothing but rubble, and if the new farmer keeps cattle they are housed elsewhere. I do not write this in a spirit of sentimentality. The National Trust appears to be doing an excellent job, and is putting the farm site to an admirable purpose. Furthermore, not even my grandfather's most loyal supporter would deny that, in spite of his successes in the showring, he had overreached himself by the end of his life. But, for all that, it would take a hard man to feel no sense of genuine sadness as he contemplated the work of half a lifetime lying in wreckage.

The children, as I said, were mystified by all this talk of 'the farm', for there was not a single tractor or animal in sight. They were, however, intrigued to see the window of the very room where I was born, and I could see that as they studied it they struggled to make the imaginative effort to reconstruct the scene. They were also very interested to have me point out the spot where I had driven my runaway tractor. This is one of the central stories in their mythology of 'when Daddy was a little boy', an era which does not hold much fascination for them, except for my moments of naughtiness. Since I was a dull and conformist child, the body of legend is thin, but the tractor story has been a longstanding favourite.

One lunchtime, while the men were out of the yard, I had been sitting, as I often did, on a motionless tractor, driving it at breakneck speed and steering it through hairpin bends, when to my horror it began to move. Slowly, but unstoppably, it rolled across the yard and only came to a halt as it hit the wall of the cow shed, thirty yards away, with an awful crunch. I fled in terror, saying nothing to my parents. Many hours later, when at last I dared to look out of the window, I found the tractor had been returned to its place and was hardly marked. I still owe my thanks to whomsoever it was that concealed my crime. This anecdote appeared in *A Father's Diary* and was one of the bits Jack relished most. He asked me to show him the precise spot where the tractor had struck the wall; indeed, he wanted to see the actual dent.

On a warm, tranquil afternoon we took the children to see Stack Rocks and the so-called Green Bridge of Wales, spectacular rock formations which stand off this coast about seven miles west of Stackpole. As usual, we adults were gasping and goggling at these truly extraordinary freaks of geology, while the children, having given them a perfunctory glance at our insistence, were wandering round the cliff head, their eyes on the ground, looking for shells and, in Jack's case, bullets. But by then he had already had his fill of extraordinary sights.

The entire Castlemartin and Bosherston headland is under the control of the Ministry of Defence, which uses it as a shooting range for tanks. As a result, the public is only allowed to walk across limited parts of it at certain times when target practice has been suspended. This situation produces a grim irony: a piece of coastline which all the guidebooks declare to be one of, if not the, most beautiful in the entire British Isles has been appropriated by the army in order to perfect humanity's most ugly activity. There is another irony attached to the place as well: under a NATO arrangement, the German army sends one of its panzer tank units to make use of our excellent facilities each autumn. The roads crossing the range and running through the surrounding villages are made eerie by notices spelt out, not in English and Welsh, but English and German.

However, our perception of these issues is not shared by Jack, who was very interested to see a pair of Second World War tanks mounted triumphantly on little concrete ramps outside the gates of the Merrion camp. But more thrilling things were yet to come. As we drove down the winding lane that leads to the car park at the cliff top, we were suddenly confronted at a crossroads by a soldier in German uniform, wielding a pair of luridly coloured ping-pong bats, who signalled us to halt. We were then treated, if that is the word, to the first truly awesome sight of the day. A dozen tanks, in full fighting order, with their lights blazing and goggled soldiers in their cockpits, roared past us at a furious speed, which their clumsy bulk and cumbersome tracks made appear all the faster. The noise was shattering, but Jack opened the window and hung out, stunned by what he was seeing and his closeness to these cherished objects of fantasy.

Having been waved on by the cheery ping-pong soldier, we then passed another unit of tanks, which were still grouped in their firing position. Standing on a concrete pad and facing out to sea, they were ranged at uniform intervals in an exact line, their elongated barrels all raised to exactly the same angle. The soldiers in charge of them were strolling about, chatting and smoking, their day's work over, but in their way these immobile, perfectly aligned machines, which were so huge and yet capable of such fine precision, were far more menacing than the ones we had seen on the move.

Knowing Jack's interest, we were noisily enthusiastic, but he remained quite silent. Tanks have been one of his obsessions ever since his boy cousins taught him how to draw them by using different sized coins to represent their many wheels. After his lesson, he begged me to buy him *The Observer's Book of Tanks*, from which he has copied innumerable pictures. But, although he has seen a few static tanks in displays, and has of course seen them in action on film, he has never been face to face with an actual working machine, especially one on its way to war, as these must have seemed to him. I think the tremendous impact made by the reality of something that had previously existed for him only in fantasy, and always within the control of his imagination, both amazed and shocked him. I felt deeply for him at that moment. (I don't know what Tilly made of the tanks. She is not much interested in them as such, though she was excited by their rumbling power as they paraded past us, and I think she was also excited on Jack's behalf.)

While holding anti-nuclear views, as does Sally, I believe we must have a conventional weaponry and trained soldiers to use it, but the sight of these monsters, at close quarters, was nevertheless repugnant. However, one of the disturbing, and stimulating, aspects of being a parent is the often alarming discrepancy that springs up between your children's obsessions and your own ideas and principles. Having lived with this for some years now, I am convinced that, providing they are not translated into cruel or destructive behaviour, your children's fantasies, however perverse in your terms, must be allowed to thrive and ride out their course. The fact is that Jack, since being a very small boy, has been persistently militaristic in his games and choice of toys, but has never, to my knowledge, shown any real violence to either his family or friends. Soldiers, their weapons, uniforms and vehicles, have always meant something profound to him. Exactly what, I have never been able fully to understand, but I am sure that in the long run his obsession will prove as harmless as it has been important, and that he should not be discouraged.

After this experience, it was not surprising that he had no eyes for the other phenomena we had brought him to see. As soon as he decently could, he began to search for bullets. I explained to him that the tanks fired enormous shells at targets far out to sea, but he was not deterred. This was not so much obstinacy on his part, as an example of the crazy misconceptions children have of relative dimensions. Despite my explanation, and despite having seen the tank's giant barrels, he was, I know, hunting for something akin to the only other 'bullets' he has ever come across, that is the spent cartridge cases which litter our woods and he collects.

My Stackpole grandfather had huge, richly veined hands. His fingers and thumbs were stout and powerful, but what made his hands truly enormous was their breadth, for the span of his palm, held flat, was easily large enough to encircle a tea plate. When I try to reconstruct my childhood memories of him, it is his hands I chiefly recall, partly because they were remarkable in their own right, but also because I was afraid to look him in the eye. Most of these memories are gathered round the ceremony of mealtimes, which was, I suppose, when he generally saw me and when he was at his most domineering. It was his presence that I, at any rate, was most conscious of, and so, rather than face him directly, I studied his hands, which in miniature I have inherited.

Despite their immensity, these hands could wield a carving knife and fork with the sweetest dexterity. He did everything with a theatrical flourish, and his performance over a roast chicken never failed to fascinate me. And when he tackled a job, he did it properly. There was no hacking or pulling: he shaved slices off the breast in perfectly proportioned wafers, and severed the joints of legs and wings with single, devastating strokes. He laid out the slices on each plate in an elegant pattern, neatly separating the white meat from the brown with a strip of crisp skin. He always adjusted his arrangement with a few delicate flicks from the point of his knife before passing on the plate for my grandmother to add the vegetables. When

59

everyone was served, he would bend over his own plate and invade it with awe-inspiring heartiness. He had a way of piling up his food on the back of his fork, which I have never seen anyone else achieve. Every part of the meal – leg, breast and skin, potato, sprout and carrot – would be stacked up in little chunks, compressed into a solid, stratified block, drenched in gravy and briskly transported to his mouth, where it would be engulfed in one cavernous bite, leaving not a scrap or drip on his moustache. Having eaten everything else, he would scoop up his gravy with his knife, flattening its blade against the plate and leaning on it with all the strength of his formidable hands as he scraped off the last spots. He invariably left his plate so clean it could have been put straight back on the shelf without being washed.

Although I have since grown to be just as robust an eater as he was, in those days I could never finish any but the smallest meals. This he saw as a weakness which he made it his business to correct by the simple method of doubling my rations. And so, while he scoured the glaze off his plate, I would still be nauseously confronting the mound of food on my overloaded plate.

At the end of each course he would bury his face in his napkin, scrub it vigorously, and looked up to scowl at my futile picking. The table would go silent, nervously awaiting his reaction.

'Why isn't the boy eating? Is he ill?'

'He doesn't eat as fast as you,' my mother would say, trying to make light of it and evade an incident. 'He's going to try and finish, aren't you?' This would be said in a half-pleading, half-menacing tone.

I would make a further wretched effort to find and force down an edible morsel, while a still more terrible silence gripped the family.

'That's the trouble with these townies. No appetite.'

I would continue to fiddle despairingly with my food, and my parents would look on, not daring to intervene. Sometimes, he would snort contemptuously and, to my unutterable relief, tell me to ring the bell summoning the maid to clear the table. But, if he were in a cantankerous mood, he would persist and demand that I clean my plate.

'It's no use mollycoddling him.'

I would slowly carry my fork to my mouth, push it in, and struggle to chew without gagging. Then the inevitable tears would begin to gush and I would be taken ignominiously from the room.

Being 'townies' was the unforgivable crime my father and I had committed: we could never compensate for it, and my grandfather would never excuse it. Now that I know more about his history, I can understand why our urbanism was so offensive to him, but at the time I was only conscious, in a child's blind way, of the injustice of being harassed for a fault I could not help. The fact was that my grandfather had himself been a towny for the greater part of his working life, and had furthermore made a successful career of it. Farming, and especially horses, had always been his love, but in 1918, in common with thousands of others, he had been forced to sell his smallholding. After a ruinous venture in the transport business, which cost him every penny he owned, he found a salaried job as a salesman with Shell in Manchester, where he worked for the next fifteen years, rising to be the manager of his district. Then, at last, he took his undoubtedly courageous decision to resign from Shell and return to farming by leasing the Home Farm, where I was born. Thus, the town had always been a prison for him, in which he had languished all those years, dreaming of the country and his old life.

But, no sooner had he shaken the vile city dust from his coat, than his beloved daughter turned round and married an incorrigible towny, a man who had not only been brought up in Liverpool, but was entirely committed to following his profession there. And it was in Liverpool that this lamentable son-in-law proceeded, not unnaturally, to bring up his son, my grandfather's only grandson. Here perhaps lay the real crime for which I was being punished: no man would have been good enough to marry his daughter, but of all unsuitable types my father, an office-bound, soft-handed, city-slicker solicitor, was the most unsuitable. My father was a disappointment to him, and his sins were visited on my head. Or so I believe. I may be wrong about all this, but it is certainly the case that I grew up to feel that I had disappointed him in some irretrievable way.

In my case, being a towny meant that I could not perform the simplest task around the farm without bungling it or bursting into tears. Unlike my grandfather, and my father for that matter, I was shy and introspective; I was also unpractical and physically unadventurous, in which I did resemble my father. (We are of course mental lions.) Though I have indulged in more than my share of folly in later life, as a child I was no more foolish than the next, but my grandfather contrived to find ways of making me look and, worse, feel a fool. All my childhood memories of him are fraught with humiliation.

On summer afternoons he would sometimes drive us in his Land Rover down to Barafundle beach, a journey that involved crossing a string of parkland fields and opening innumerable five-bar gates, a job which was given to me. It was my grandfather's idea of a joke to leave me behind at each gate, forcing me to run after the car until he slowed down and allowed me to clamber aboard just before I had to get out again to attend to the next gate. I don't know how often he played this trick on me; perhaps a couple of times, perhaps only once, perhaps never, yet although it was hardly an act of gross sadism it has stuck in my mind as a very bitter memory.

He was not a cruel man, but he was certainly not 'kind', in

the sense my children use the word to describe certain adults they like. This has nothing to do with generosity. (My grandfather was most generous, always loading our car for the return journey to Liverpool with more food and presents than we could comfortably carry.) An adult who regularly gave my children sweets would win their warmest attention, but would not necessarily win the title of 'kindness'. By this I think they mean a willingness to accept them on their terms and take an interest in them as they are, without patronizing them or standing on adult dignity. It is a mysterious fact that some people, who strike the adult eye as being the very picture of avuncular warmth, have the effect of repelling children, while others, who are seemingly cold and dull, are adored by them. These latter, though they may never part with a single sweet or coin, are nevertheless 'kind', for they possess an affinity with children, an instinctive identification with their way of seeing the world. My grandfather, despite being considered a jovial and benign figure by his friends, lacked this special quality; at any rate, he did in his dealings with me.

He never understood that his jokes did far more than make fun of me, they crushed me. I may well have been wet for my age, too prone to tears, and spoilt by an overpossessive mother, but his teasing, far from giving me backbone and toughening me up, only rendered me a thousand times the wetter, because it stripped me of everything, even the power to sulk. His jibes rubbed me out: I felt literally erased, reduced to empty space. It never occurred to me to call his bluff and stay at the gate, making him come back for me: I simply ran, hating his laughter, hating the others for laughing too, hating my own incompetence.

Oddly enough, however, I did not hate him. As children do, I distinguished between the man and his deeds, hating what he did to me, while still continuing to love, or at least feel good about, 'Grandpa' himself. I have noticed in my children this same ability to split the horrible parts of one's behaviour from the nice parts, and thus keep faith with their version of the person they love. It seems that children will forgive almost anything, even the foulest cruelty, but what they cannot withstand is the steady undermining of their sense of their own worth, their dignity, and nothing undermines it more effectively than mockery, constant mockery. To jeer at a child is to put him in a cupboard, and is just as cruel; to make a practice of jeering at him is to lock him up and throw away the key.

From the point of view of natural history, our trip to the other end of the Castlemartin shooting range, at St Govan's Head, was the greater success. Protesting vociferously at the dreadful prospect of 'going for a walk', the children were herded along the coast path until we reached the first of the many faults that incise these cliffs. This one has not acquired a name, perhaps because of its forbidding appearance. It is in the shape of a three-sided dock, its fourth side open to the sea, which in size could easily accommodate a small ship. Its two-hundred-foot walls are sheer and uniform, and the water in its basin is always dark and fathomless. Most of the faults, stacks and arches here possess an inspiring grandeur, inducing feelings which in the eighteenth century would have been termed sublime, but this straight-lined, shadowed, chilly, open-ended giant's grave is, for all its enormity, repellent.

We hurried on to the famous Huntsman's Leap, another fault reaching deep into the cliff, which at its sea end is almost closed by two walls so close together a man once jumped across on his horse. Having performed this feat, the intrepid huntsman is then said to have looked back and died of shock. Legend does not record the psychological state of his horse.

Jack was very puzzled by this folk tale.

'Where did the horse jump?' he kept asking me. 'Why did the man die?'

As we stood peering into the abyss, we suddenly noticed a black head bobbing in the water. The binoculars soon showed it to be a seal. The tide was low, but coming in, and the swell, concentrated by the narrow neck of the gorge, was surging with a forceful push and pull motion. The seal, however, rode the water languidly, never getting near the rock walls. It swam upright, in what seemed to us a curious posture, its head lying back. At first, we thought it was trapped, or ill, or exhausted, but having since seen other, manifestly fit seals swimming in just the same way I now know it was simply basking. They appear to dislike the sun, positively seeking out these cold, gloomy spots for their relaxation.

Its neck was richly wrinkled, like the neck of a Berlin plutocrat in a Grosz cartoon, and it wore the moustache of an ageing bounder. Its colouring was very striking, for its corpulent torpedo of a body was mottled by the very colours of the pebbles in our cove when they have been darkened and polished by the tide – sea greens and blues of every dark hue, mixed with limestone grey. Occasionally, it would make an idle dive, disappearing for a couple of minutes, and then surfacing to blow its bristles dry and roll indolently with the waves.

The children were thrilled. However, standing at the far end of the fault, we were obliged to lean over the edge at a sickening angle in order to observe the seal. All of us felt the effects of vertigo, except Tilly who had still learnt no fear of these cliffs. She skittered on the crumbling brink with all the oblivious unconcern of the rabbits we had disturbed. I really feared for her. Though dainty and graceful in repose, in motion she is chaotic and often trips headlong over the most insignificant obstacles. We warned her, and shouted at her again and again, but she is uncontrollably vivacious, never standing still for a moment. Indeed, most of this last summer she has seldom been seen the right way up, having become an habitual cartwheeler and performer of headstands. Fortunately, she did not give way to gymnastics that afternoon.

Jack, on the other hand, shares my terror of heights, and stood well back behind the line of sight; I don't think he can have seen the seal more than once, though he was very interested.

'Come back, come back,' he implored me, every time I approached the edge, dragging at my clothes.

Bullets were still on his mind as we walked back and, by dint of combing the path, never once lifting his eyes, he finally found something that might well have been a .22 shell. But Sally was horrified and threw it away before I had a chance to inspect it.

On their return home, I was put under strict orders by Jack to find him a bullet, and by Tilly to return to Huntsman's Leap to make sure the seal was 'still happy'.

Our holiday is over. Sally and the children have left, and I have moved from the Granary to the smaller Farm Cottage, where I must try to write about our discoveries of the last seven days. From my new bedroom window, when the tide is up, I can see the crests of waves breaking on the biggest rocks in the cove. This coming and going of the water, seen from the window, creates the odd illusion that it is the earth tilting, and not the tide rising and falling, which brings the waves in and out of view. The tide invests time with a rhythm that is independent of night and day, a rhythm that does not rest in the dark or need daylight for its work, but throbs to its own impatient clock. And I can feel that same clock tugging and pushing my energy now I am alone, and no longer subject to an ordinary, domestic timetable.

I confess that as the family drove away I felt a lurch of self-pity and more than a twinge of fear, for I suddenly realized that I had never before spent a week on my own. I have either lived with my parents, in schools, in digs with other people, or in homes of my own with various partners, and during my entire forty-one years there has never been a single interlude of solitariness. For the first time, I was to be exposed to my own exclusive company, and I did not relish the prospect.

My instinctive response to being marooned on the island of myself was to go shopping and stock up with consoling luxuries. On my return, I threw my bags on the sofa, only to find that I had buried Sophie, a doll Tilly had left behind to keep me company. Not that one is allowed to refer to this personage as a doll: she is 'daughter', 'sister' or 'friend' to Tilly, but never a doll. Before departing, Tilly had given me elaborate instructions concerning Sophie's treatment and routine: she was to sleep in the bed next to mine, in her nightdress, she was to be dressed in the morning, put out if the sun shone, given a nap in the afternoon, and to be regularly fed. I admit that at the time I only listened to this catalogue with half an ear, but when I saw her buried face-down beneath my shopping, and unmistakably reduced to being a doll, I was stricken with guilt. Conscious of my foolishness, I rescued her and propped her up on a cushion, as ordered. And there she has sat, her dignity intact, ever since.

As instructed, I returned to Bosherston in search of seals and bullets. It was a perfect evening, still, very warm and a little misty, giving the setting sun the moist look of a peeled orange. Cruelly, the weather has done nothing but improve since Sally and the children left. The red flag was down to show that shooting had finished for the day, but I found I had the entire headland to myself, for mine was the only car parked and there were no other walkers on the coast path.

I walked on to the first fault in the cliffs, shaped like a dock, but neither here, nor at Huntsman's Leap did I see a seal. A further half mile or so brought me to a point overlooking a natural arch in the cliffs, which though not as spectacular or photogenic as the famous Green Bridge of Wales, nonetheless moved me deeply. A substantial arm of rock, resembling a sort of collapsed pier, reaches into the sea, gradually sloping down to the waves, and a gap has been eaten away in the thickest section close to the main cliff. Perhaps in half a million years or so it will have developed into a sight as popular and awesome as the Green Bridge. At the moment, however, it offers a different kind of satisfaction, for longer inspection removes the idea of a pier, and suggests instead a cathedral, or at any rate a curious version of ecclesiastical architecture, from which the exterior walls have dropped away. The arch itself rises and falls in a majestic Romanesque curve, such as one might expect standing between nave and chancel, and revealed beyond is a dappled light that might have fallen through the stained glass of an east window.

Church analogies really are impossible to avoid. The face of the cliff is indented with a series of gracefully arched caves: the largest, a shadowy, mysterious chamber, looks like a lady chapel built into the long transept that stretches out to sea; some, which are taller and shallower, look like niches designed to hold the attenuated statues of saints; and the smallest ones, a line of low recesses, might have been installed to display the tombs of kings and bishops. The whole structure is supported and decorated by pillars gathered in slender clusters round a huge, central column, or standing singly and branching into fantastic ribbed vaults. The style of this extraordinary cliff is, in a word, Gothic, for as with churches built in highest Gothic its entire surface is thickly encrusted with ornament: the canopies of the tombs are elaborately carved, little figures and strange shapes proliferate in the vaulting, and every arch is underhung with ornate mouldings. And continually washing in and out of these ecclesiastical caves is the sea, which like a fanatical craftsman cannot leave its creation alone, but is forever reshaping and rebuilding it, until in the end the whole glorious edifice will collapse beneath its indefatigable chisel.

Some cliffs yield smoothly to the sea and wind, eroding gradually and leaving no trace of their diminution, but these magnificent Bosherston rocks make an exhibition of their great raw bones and their treacherous soft streaks. The story of their battle with existence is immediately legible in their forms. Tide by tide, year by year, millenium by millenium, the waves lick away their flesh, probing their faults, prizing apart their fissures, and grinding down even their toughest parts. The all-destroying sea must win, but the rocks do not concede their inevitable decline with grace or dignity. They fight to survive and, like us, they bring to the struggle a contradictory mix of strength and weakness. Like us, they strive to resist the irresistible. The record of their doomed efforts is inscribed in the broken body of this Gothic peninsula, with its demolished and abandoned buttresses, its tottering pillars, cavernous openings and rotting walls. And I also saw figured in this ruin the relic of a mind: here hope had been disappointed, strength thwarted, and will-power undermined, but, for all that, here too was a heroic monument to endurance.

Returning from my cathedral and its congregation of lethal waves, I walked as a child does, ignoring the view and concentrating on the ground at my feet. I was rewarded. Not far from the little guard house where the red warning flag is hoisted and lowered, I found the dented brass nose of a spent bullet. I will wrap it and send it on to Jack.

*

69

My grandfather's farm incorporated two beaches, which are now also in the care of the National Trust. The closest to the farmhouse is Broadhaven, whose name derives from its huge, triangular expanse of sand. We walked there after our dispiriting visit to the Home Farm, taking the path that runs along the bank of one of the lily ponds. There are three of these pools, and they reach into the mainland like the toes of a claw. Once they were tidal inlets, but in the eighteenth century the Cawdor family dammed them up to create freshwater pools for fishing, bathing and boating – and for the sake of their sheer beauty. The trees along the bank were festooned with the feathery plumes of Old Man's Beard, and although it was too late in the season to see any flowers, the extraordinary abundance of pads on the water showed why these ponds are famous for their summer displays of lilies.

At the far end of these pools, where they join at the ankle, as it were, there is a venerable limestone bridge, built wide enough to carry a horse and cart, and here I used to sit as a boy, resting after what seemed to me the marathon walk from our house, and staring into the clear water in the hope of seeing a pike. Having no predators to attack them, these creatures are said to enjoy measureless longevity and attain monstrous proportions. I never saw but one, and that was not so large, yet it moved with ominous authority. It glided sluggishly in and out of the weeds clinging to the side of the bridge, its murderous jaw hung slightly open to reveal its trap of teeth, which, so I was told, were like pigs' teeth in that they curved backwards and would never let a victim loose.

The lily ponds feed a small stream which flows along the cliff wall enclosing the beach, making it possible to build canal systems in the sand and provide castles with proper moats, whatever the state of the tide. Out at sea is a curiously shaped rock, which from a certain angle exactly resembles a spired church. It looks reasonably close to the shore, because the intervening span of sea, being flat, deludes the eye. Having been told that it was too dangerous to be swum round, I was fascinated by this rock. I longed for someone to make the attempt, and one memorable afternoon a couple did so. A crowd gathered to cheer them off – and warn them. The girl wore a white swimsuit, and waved to us, standing in the water. They struck out for the rock, and soon even their bobbing heads had vanished. Twenty minutes later, the girl dragged herself out of the sea, begging people to help her friend. He was rescued alive, but as he was carried up the beach we could see that his back had been appallingly scourged, as if by a cat-o'-nine-tails. We were told he had been overpowered by the current. The rock had won, as I knew it would.

Apart from possessing every facility required of a classic holiday beach – cliffs, rocks, pools, caves, dunes and fine sand – Broadhaven also has the inestimable advantage of being within walking distance of Violet and Don's Ye Olde World Cottage Cafe. However, as a child, I preferred the other beach, Barafundle Bay, which though smaller is if anything more spectacular. Nowadays, the beach is approached by a flight of steps leading down the sheer face of its cliff wall, and it was while making this familiar descent one hot afternoon, the hottest, we were told, of the entire miserable season, that I felt the closest connection between the children and my childhood self.

In part, this was owing to the banal fact that all children tend to behave the same way on beaches. Tilly and Jack ran, whooping, down the steps, and having no bathing costumes, they were soon prancing at the edge of the sea in their pants, taunting and screaming at the waves as they rolled in to splash their legs. They built a formidable sandcastle, complete with moat, drawbridge and a multitude of tumbling, bucket-sized turrets, and when the tide began to destroy it they worked with doomed frenzy to repair its melting walls. They combed the tide-line for treasure; they gathered wood for our fire; they poked their fingers into anenomes to feel their furry clutch; they tried to kick limpets off their rocks; they made caves echo with ghostly shouts. In short, they fulfilled every time-honoured tradition of the beach.

Later, as we were having lunch, they withdrew to a long slope of sand dune behind us, where they constructed a sort of Cresta Run for some round stones they had collected. They scooped out a serpentine channel in the sand, marked its angles with smaller pebbles, and sent their stones rolling down. This they did for twenty minutes or more, concentrating on the game to the point of being deaf and blind to everything else.

It was the obsessive, endlessly repetitive quality of their game that brought me closely in touch with my own childhood, for I can vividly recall being preoccupied for hours at a time with games that consisted in little more than reiterated ritual. From the outside such games seem transparent and readily explicable, and indeed many are just so. I remember coming home from seeing Bertram Mills Circus in Liverpool's Sefton Park and standing in the bathroom with a chair in my hand, defying the man-eating lions which prowled round the bath mat, their tails lashing. With a towel round my shoulders and a flannel on my head, I was gorgeously costumed in the spangled cape and braided cap of the lion-tamer I had just clapped until my hands hurt. Anyone who had walked in on me at that moment would have had no difficulty in recognizing the purely imitative side of this game. Its pleasure obviously derived from the adopted glamour and skill of the real lion-tamer. Yet it had its ritualized side too: the lions prowled in a ceaseless round, and the tamer had them perform the same trick over and over again.

But other games are not so palpable. To a casual observer, the little boy may appear to be doing nothing more than trundling his truck up and down the carpet, making motor noises; however, what the adult cannot perceive, and the child cannot express, is the aura of fantasy emanating from the truck and its movements. Speaking for myself – one can do no more – the fantasies associated with my repetitive games were beyond expression, because they did not take the form of imitated or invented scenarios, which I acted out and could have described if I had suddenly been invested with adult powers of articulation. They were instead a state of mind, or, rather, an emotional tone, which was sustained and strengthened by the rhythm of the ritual. When being a cowboy, for instance, it was sufficient simply to run around with a galloping motion, clapping a hand to my buttocks, making clicking noises and occasionally firing off a few rounds. I was in a trance, a state of deep meditation around the theme of cowboy. For an only child, these games have a hermetic quality not attained by siblings, though I noticed that in spite of their running commentary Tilly and Jack played with their stones like sleepwalkers, their minds turned inwards.

I think people who live on their own must go slightly mad; at any rate, I feel I am going mad here in this cottage. I am so unused to solitude, but after only three days I have come to detest my own presence. I feel as if I have been imprisoned with no one for company but my own unutterably predictable, tediously familiar self. I want someone to report the day to, someone to amuse and be amused by, someone to cook for and eat with, someone to break the unending monotony of me. And yet, I am so impatient towards those I do live with. I am angry with Sally and the children, who have done nothing to deserve it; I hate myself for being cold and odious, but I cannot find a cure. How is this circle to be broken?

Every morning and afternoon I take the path that leads from my cottage, up a steep bank until I am almost standing on the cottage roof, and up towards the cliff head where its edges are splashed with the sulphurous tints of toadflax. Along this path it is possible to stand at the exact point where the rock changes from limestone's grey to sandstone's crumbling pink. Here, on a clear day, you can see Stackpole Head, which juts out beyond Barafundle Bay, and to the east, much further away, you can see the ruins of Manorbier Castle, which was surely built for pleasure rather than defence, for it stands right on the beach. And below my feet, two hundred feet below, the sea meets the land, tirelessly besieging it, using its own rocks to batter its foundations and bring down the cliff wall.

And yet it is impossible not to see a sensual relationship between the sea and the rocks. The tide makes its irresistible approach, caressing the recumbent stone, fondling the seaweed hair, tonguing and penetrating the soft parts, forcing its way into crevices and fissures, agitating the walls of tunnels and caves with its slow, urgent rhythms and sudden spasms of creamy spume. And after its reluctant withdrawal, it leaves behind a spending of liquid life in the wombs of rock pools. Yet male and female are interchangeable in this eternal loveplay. Though the rocks are doomed in the end to melt and shrink in the sea's moist grasp, they protrude for the time being, pushing their fingers and peninsulas into the sea's yielding depths, demanding the waves' sucking embrace, and impelling the water to enclose and release them as it rises and falls in its lunar cycle. This inexhaustible dalliance is forever forming and reforming their gender. The stack rocks, standing today so massively erect, their shafts plunged in the sea's lapping clasp, were only yesterday, in geological time, the gently rounded arches through which the rampant waves surged with every thrust of the tide. Perhaps this union of dissolving solids and adamantine liquids is the metaphor of true marriage, in which male and female are transcended to create a single, wholly fulfilled being.

I don't know how far landscape may be said to make character, but it can certainly symbolize it. I have discovered that the landscape of my birthplace is animated by the same forces that prevail in my mind, which indeed seems to be an extension, a dislodged fragment, of this contradictory coast. Inside my head, the same winds blow, the same currents drive, the same tides ebb and flow, mysterious powers that are never exposed or understood, but never cease to have their effect as they chafe and shake the rocks of my consciousness. The more I walk this coast path, the more compulsively I identify with the particular combination of hard and soft, strength and weakness, that is the distinctive feature of Stackpole's geology. I identify with the doomed obstinacy of the stack rocks, but I also feel within myself a dangerous similarity to the long, open, supine stretches of beach, which offer no resistance to the sea and lie submissively beneath the tide's energy. I see myself, or rather I see my lack of self in the ever-shifting sand dunes, which never fix and build themselves, but are continually resculpted by every wind that puffs. These are the male and female in me, constantly blending, constantly at war, constantly being remade, without ever settling into a finished form.

This pairing, without union, of endurance and surrender, duty and indulgence, truth and dishonesty, which seem to be the irreconcilable elements of my formless character, are summed up in the very name of my birthplace. Stack comes evidently from the Norse *stac*, meaning an isolated rock, while Pole comes from *pollr*, meaning small inlet. The rock itself, carboniferous limestone, is infected with this deadly marriage of hard and soft, which produces the great tusks of durable stone and their underlying grottoes and arches.

Walking back along the cliff path, with the breaking rock at my feet, the wind in my nose, the sea in my ears and eyes, I long to put an end to this confusion and win some peace of mind for all of us. I want to be the rock on which Sally can rely, and the sea that will seduce and possess her; I want to be the cliff where my children can nest and grow in safety, and also the tide that sets in motion the moons of their imagination. I want to be a husband and father, and stop my never-ending quest for self.

This is my last night here in the cottage, and it is late. The guns at Castlemartin have been pounding all day, sometimes sending tiny shock waves across the surface of my whisky, and tonight the tide is booming in the cove below. I have just walked down to the rocks to look at the water, but the night is very black and without a torch I could only see the occasional flash of white spray. My case is packed, the cottage is clean, and I am ready to leave tomorrow. Now, however, for the last time I must try to make sense of this trip.

I am forced to conclude that, on the whole, my idea of rediscovering my childhood self, and learning more about my children by returning them to the site of so many of my holidays, has proved unproductive. Only once did I experience a moment of illumination when I thought I detected a melting together of memory and the present in the common essence of childhood, and that was at the beach. My own childhood had not been revived. The memories I have of Stackpole are ones I already had, which have been strengthened but not added to by our experiment. I seem to be shackled to the here and now, and cannot break free.

We went to look at my grandparents' grave, which lies behind the church at Stackpole Elidor, just to the north of Quay Farm. The children sat on the modest tomb while I photographed them, and then they gathered up some of the coloured marble chips for their collection of 'precious jewels'. It was only as I read the memorial lettering round the stone – Constance Charlotte Bennion, died 17 November 1958 – that I realized, with a shock, I had no real memories of my grandmother, and none had been stimulated in the last few days. And yet she, of all my grandparents, was probably the kindest to me and the most sympathetic to children in general. She had been a teacher. Certainly, she understood the position my grandfather used to put me in, and did not like it. 'Leave the child alone, John!' she would say when the mealtime ordeal was reaching its tearful denouement. I do not remember his ever doing as she asked, but I was thankful for her gesture all the same. She was generous with presents and, as far as I recall, always had time for me. I was fourteen when she died, and away at school, but I have no memory of the event, nor even of being saddened. Why should this be? It seems so unjust that he, the tyrant, should be remembered, while she, the comforter, should be forgotten. But memory does not deal in justice: it seems to nurse grudges and honour cheap greats, while obliterating true charity.

It is too late. I can't go on. I have lost faith in what I am writing. My journey has failed.

NOVEMBER

The crisis which had been gathering all summer finally broke in November, and in a fit of what now seems to have been madness I decided to leave home.

On that particular day, Sally was due to be out of the house all afternoon, and I planned to tell her of my decision in the evening, after the children had gone to bed, so as to be gone by the time they woke next morning. As it happened, Sally returned, around six o'clock, with Jack alone, having left Tilly to stay the night with a friend. However, I was too agitated to handle the situation properly and with unforgivable clumsiness I blurted out my plan in Jack's hearing. Sally immediately collapsed in a chair and began to sob. Seeing that we were having a row, but not realizing its gravity, his first response was agonizingly flippant.

'Why don't you get divorced then?' he demanded, in an exasperated tone.

I struggled to close down the discussion until he was in bed, but by then Sally was too distressed to control her crying and Jack was too curious. We were therefore forced to play out a grotesque travesty of an ordinary family evening. I had cooked roast chicken with roast potatoes, one of Jack's favourite meals, and since he was hungry I had no choice but to serve it and go through the motions of having supper with him. Sally remained in her chair, unable to eat, unable to move. I sat at the table with Jack and for a while the horror of my imminent going was overlaid with the usual chatter and routine of getting a child to eat. I unscrewed the cap of the tomato ketchup, told him off for spilling it on the table, made him eat his carrots and forced him to eat two last mouthfuls before leaving the table. Though he glanced continuously at Sally's broken figure, he ate heartily enough.

Sally roused herself and took him for a bath. She got him into his pyjamas and put him to bed, asking him to stay upstairs so we could talk. He bravely agreed, but was down in the sitting room before we had begun. Hoping to reassure him, Sally explained that Daddy was going away for a little while 'to think about his work'; she told him not to worry and tried to get him to bed once more. Sally and I managed to talk for a minute or two, but then we heard a noise outside the door and he had to be brought in.

By now he had grasped the dire nature of what was happening. He ran to Sally, who was sitting on the sofa opposite me, and hugged her, both to comfort her and reassure himself. Next, he ran to me and sat on my knee, but sensing that I would not yield he returned to Sally. From her lap, he begged me not to go. I left the room.

When I came back, I found him peering anxiously through the curtains into the darkness, looking for the taxi which Sally had told him would take me away.

'Don't go, Daddy. Send the taxi back.'

I told him I had to go, but that I would come home soon.

Sally was still crying, and for a moment he became angry.

'I'm going to chop you up,' he said, 'and make a new Daddy that won't go.'

I repeated that I had to go and he began to cry at last. He ran to and fro between us, refusing to go to bed. However, despite his tears, he did not for a moment give up his efforts to persuade me to stay. Throughout the whole nightmare, his attitude was resolutely constructive and he never once acceded to the adult arrangements made over his head. Again and again he went to the window, as if to keep the taxi at bay by his vigilance.

Finally, Sally took him upstairs and lay with him in our bed until he fell asleep. She told me he had been crossing his fingers in the hope that I would not drive off in the taxi.

An hour later I went upstairs to see if he was really asleep. He lay open-mouthed and quietly snoring, his fingers still staunchly crossed. I looked at him for a long while, but felt no wavering in my determination. Shortly afterwards, I left the house.

I stayed away for four days, putting Sally through a season in hell, and I am writing this less than a fortnight after my return. The effects of my desertion will be felt by all of us, especially Sally, for many months to come. The flaws in our marriage, which have been so traumatically exposed, will have to be faced, understood, and if possible mended. At the moment, however, I understand nothing. I did a dreadful thing to Sally and the children, but I came home and was given a welcome I did not deserve. I only know that I am more confused than callous, and that in my bungling way I do love them.

Those four days were spent in a part of Norfolk which was strikingly beautiful, but, to my impressionable eye, painfully symbolic of our situation.

Spread around the cottage was a rich agricultural estate, rich enough to have kept unharmed many of the paddocks and meadows close to the main house, while farming the rest of its acres as intensively as possible. The view from my windows was a flat, unbroken expanse of sugar beet, furrows and winter barley, which was just beginning to throw a blush of green over the smooth, frost-bound earth. It was an empty farmscape, devoid of animals and machinery, the land having been left to work out its winter fertility. The only life to be seen was provided by lapwings scattered across on the bare soil and continually rising in alarm at threats I could not see to make their shrill 'pee-wit' call. Ditches, shorn of their hedges, cut the land into an irregular pattern, ornamenting it with silver streaks wherever water lay in their grooves. The few trees that remained were mostly confined to the far horizon. In one of the meadows near the house the corrugated relics of an ancient village were visible: the broad furrow of an ancient roadway, the rectangular ditches of a moat that might have surrounded a manor house, and one or two house platforms, could easily be picked out. The sunken track wound its way across the old grass, but was abruptly cut off at one end by the margin of a cultivated field, from which all trace of the lost village had long since been obliterated by ploughing. In the evenings, the setting sun hung over all this like a smoking lamp in the sky, throwing up a great canopy of coloured fumes, while below, the turning autumn trees burned still more fiercely in its chill glow. The whole estate seemed to be ignited by a single, brilliant flame, whose smouldering mist thickened the darkness.

Thus, the landscape could be read as an eloquent tangle of continuity and broken tradition, of new growth and old life uprooted. But how did all this apply to my life, to my children? Was my family to be abandoned and dispersed, like a lost village, leaving nothing behind it except the overgrown marks of its empty site? Or would fresh life spring up to embrace the past and grow with it, keeping everything alive in a new, if damaged, form?

For the past five years of my working life, I have tried to translate our experience back into the language of natural symbolism, seeing in nature the most meaningful images of our struggle to endure with dignity in the face of mortality and unavoidable suffering. It has become almost an article of faith with me that, just as natural life requires a secure environment in which to flourish at its richest, so does the human personality; just as new life is the product of old soil, so tradition is the only matrix capable of bearing true creativity. The Gothic church and the oak tree, as I mentioned before, have come to stand in my mind as the great twin symbols of this rooted strength of form, which alone possesses the power to adapt and innovate, to reinvigorate the old with the new. For me, an aged oak whose maimed limbs are still shooting with fresh foliage is a living metaphor of our human capacity to survive, with our creativity intact, the onslaughts of failure, loss, pain and all the other trials existence inflicts on life. It speaks too of our refusal to give up hope, our refusal to give up the fight to remake the imagination. And, since our Welsh holiday, I have found another symbol of this flawed tenacity in the embattled rocks of Bosherston, with which I feel my personal history is even more closely associated.

And yet, despite my beliefs, here I was contemplating the destruction of my own roots and history. The children would of course survive, but what scars would they bear? What distortions would be imposed on their growth? Looking at this melancholy landscape, whose every feature seemed to confirm the truth of my convictions, I could not understand how I had reached the point where I was not only in danger of making nonsense of my work, but of relinquishing what had for the last ten years been my most precious belonging – my family. Was I discovering that the love of children could be as changeable as sexual love? Surely, this could not be so? It seemed a perversion of nature. Could parental love evaporate as suddenly and mysteriously as the mist that coiled and billowed outside my window every morning, and then vanished to leave the ground naked and spare? Or, could everything be united, after all, in a ramshackle harmony, within the grasp of love, fused together as the broken parts of this countryside were by the soft, liquid light of the November sun?

It is one of the many tragedies of our day that we, as a generation of parents, have lost our way. We no longer understand our role, nor the role in the future for which we are preparing our children. The old liberalism of the 1960s (and I speak as a product of that heady era), the belief that feelings must be honoured and nurtured above all else, has manifestly failed, bequeathing nothing but a welter of divorce and fractured families. On the other hand, the new call for discipline and authoritarianism, apart from striking us as repugnant, does not seem any more relevant to a world which offers the next generation so little in the way of creative occupation, and threatens so much in the way of sadism, destruction and incoherence.

The problem runs much deeper than chronic and widespread unemployment, though that is obviously the imprisoning condition of many people's lives, and must sap the confidence of even the most pragmatic parent. The hopelessness and apathy which, as a part-time teacher, I have seen in so many sixth-formers' faces, cannot be solely attributed to the fears they hold regarding their careers, for they, after all, stand the best chance of winning the few available jobs. No, we confront a far more serious crisis, one of values and ideals, and the indifference of these sixth-formers to their own fate and that of the world is perhaps the result of their apprehending, at the last moment, the cultural vacuum we have left them in place of a future. We no longer have a social ideal to hold up for them to strive after or reject; we have no communally shared moral or political goal; we have no vision of an improved future, which we have brought them up to enhance and realize. We do not know what kind of world we ought to be constructing, and therefore we do not know how to be parents. For, clearly, childhood is a meaningless episode if it is not received as the prelude to a fulfilled adulthood.

One of the paradoxical effects of this void is that we have fallen back on the conviction that, in lieu of anything more positive, we must encourage our children to fulfil themselves as children. As a result, this is the golden age of childhood. Never before has so much attention been lavished on the imaginative and sensuous life of children. But this highly developed faculty for self-expression, together with a vague emphasis on tolerance of others, is the sum of our parental gift. Our children are being trained to express themselves and their creativity to the full, yet they are being given nothing to express; nothing, that is, in the sense of a defined and generally accepted model of the self. We lack any idea of the good person, the good citizen, even of the good worker. We are parents without authority; indeed, we have passed it to our children, who now unwittingly dictate the terms of their own upbringing. Whatever needs they show must at all costs be provided for. However, there is more to this than mere indulgence: in a world fraught with violence and sterility, we value our children, like our wildlife, for their unspoilt beauty and uncorrupted creativity, and we do all we can to cultivate these qualities within the fragile environment of the family. In a world where the adult is nothing, the child has become everything, and the parent has been demoted to a lovingly attentive protector.

This concentration on the nurturing side of parenthood

87

would be ideal, if it were rooted in some notion of instruction and the inculcation of values. However, since it is not, it places a crushing burden on those for whom love does not flow readily, or for whom love is problematic. Like most parents, I have my own code of priorities, which I attempt to pass on to my children, though I am all too conscious that it is arbitrary and personal, and that it is not backed by any social consensus. There is no such thing as a private morality; or rather, there is, but by its very nature it cannot be taught, it can only be put up as a solitary, disconnected option. In the absence of a communally agreed morality to fall back on for support, such personal visions of the world and the way it ought to be lived in can only be effectively conveyed by means of love, and if for some reason love stumbles or is stifled the parent is robbed of authority and can do nothing.

Looking back over my life in the unaccustomed silence of that childless Norfolk cottage, I felt it could be read as a history of ever-recurring rupture. There seemed to be a deeply structured flaw in my character, like a geological fault, which had first split the surface in childhood and had continued to crack open at intervals, devastating whatever had been built over it in the meanwhile. This lethal flaw has often lain dormant for long periods, giving every appearance of stability, and allowing new life to settle and flourish over its deceptive seam, and then, usually without warning, but always with terrible violence, the crack has widened and yawned again, burying everything above in rubble and ruin, swallowing up all the reconstruction of previous years.

When I married Sally and we had our children, I thought that my volcanic fissure had at last been sealed over, that its sides had closed and steadied for good, leaving nothing but an old scar on the crust, which would in time be erased beneath the topsoil of our family life. But, evidently, I had been deluded, for the crevasse was shifting once more, and Sally and I were left clinging to its opposing edges. Was this really an incorrigible defect in my personality, or were we experiencing, in an extreme form, something which every marriage is bound to undergo at one time or another?

When I tried to think back and locate the first, undetected tremblings of this earthquake, they seemed to date from the time when we moved from Street Farm, Stowlangtoft, to our present house. This took place in July 1984, a year and two months after the end of the period described in *A Father's Diary*. There was an unavoidable symbolism to be seen in the contrast of our first house with the second. Street Farm, which more than any other house since my chidhood had been 'home', was in both a physical and social sense closely associated with the village and the life of its farm, whereas our present house, though beautifully sited, has no firm connection with any village, and is quite distant from the farm whose land it occupies. We have no immediate neighbours, we stand within the boundaries of one parish, while overlooking another, we take our postal address and telephone exchange from a third village, we shop in a fourth, drink in a fifth and send our children to school in a sixth. Our life here is, in a word, dispersed.

Nevertheless, we had excellent reasons for moving. Sally and the children wasted no time in making up their minds to come here once we were offered the chance. I, however, hesitated, reserving my decision, which, now I come to think of it, I have yet to declare. Though based entirely on instinct, my misgivings were well-founded, because uprooting ourselves from Street Farm and moving here, a deportation of two miles at the most, turned out to be a profoundly unsettling experience.

Worst of all, I found that once in our new house my feelings for the children cooled and deteriorated. I cannot put dates to this process, or attach it to any event; I only know that it happened slowly, but inexorably. Their claims on my time and energy began to seem importunate; their little ways ceased to be charming and eccentric, becoming instead infuriatingly self-centred. Their incessant noise was no longer a merry chorus to our household life, but a clamorous and grating din; their clothes and toys seemed to gather in every room, like heaps of trash, turning the place into a slum; their questions no longer interested me; their games bored me; their jokes irritated me; their presence became intrusive and their very existence became a burden.

This sorry state of affairs coincided with a very bad patch in my work. At the best of times I find myself having to make titanic intellectual efforts to squeeze forth ideas, which only turn out to be banal and unusable. At such moments, the chaos inside my head would be made doubly intolerable if I met with chaos outside my room. When things are going well, the jolly turbulence of a family house seems to add zest to creativity, but when they go badly, as they did then for week after week, the mere sight of the children, never mind their demands on me, is enough to destroy all the mental clarity I have struggled for so laboriously at my desk. I found that there was simply not enough of me to go round. I lacked the resources to spread myself any thinner; they were thin enough when applied to my work, but when other calls were made on them, it seemed to me they would cover nothing at all. Tilly would bring me her homework and I would put her off until, to my relief, she would take the initiative and do it on her own. Jack would bring me toys to glue and I would deliberately leave them unmended in the hope that he would forget. Even now, despite everything, I am neglecting a picture of his, which he asked me to put in a frame weeks ago.

All this disturbed me deeply and exacerbated my guilt. I was revolted by my egocentrism, but could not break free of its grip. I do not know whether my tendency to feel guilty is more or less pathological than others', but I do know that my entire life has been overshadowed by guilt about something: money, for example, and my inability to earn more and spend less; work, and my chronic failure to write quicker and better; Sally, and my inattentiveness; and so on. Since the children were born, much of this futile energy has been expended on them. When I am with them, I feel guilty about my lack of patience; when I am not with them, I feel guilty about my negligence. Guilt is no doubt a condition of being human, and perhaps in parents it helps to stimulate our protective instincts. Yet it is one of the most fruitless emotions, for, as often as not, its only effect is to paralyse, preventing whatever is wrong from being put right, and thus causing still more guilt.

But, for all that, neither our move here, however disorienting, nor the difficulties I was having with my work seemed sufficient reasons in themselves for my dissociation from the children. Had love itself failed? Was I imprisoned in selfishness? I could not believe it. There had to be a way back to my old devotion. Or, perhaps, the only way to take now was towards a new devotion? For surely love was not entirely spontaneous and arbitrary? Surely it could be animated by the will?

And so, in the crystal dark of those Norfolk nights, with Halley's comet wheeling unseen above me, I struggled to find a foothold in the other, clouded darkness of the chasm that had opened up beneath us.

From the moment I returned home, Jack waged an energetic campaign to bring Sally and me together and keep us that way.

As on the dreadful night of my leaving, his approach was unshakeably positive. Whenever Sally and I were in the same room, talking, he would come in again and again to check our mood and ask if we were 'all right'. His vigilance did not slacken for many days, until he was sure no further sign of separation was developing between us. He stayed as close to me as he could, sometimes just clinging to my leg or holding my hand, and sometimes demanding to give me a full-blooded hug and kiss. He often tried to hug both of us in a single all-enfolding embrace, which his small arms could not really achieve. He also became extremely attentive to us, running to serve our needs as soon as the smallest wish was indicated.

Though occasionally prone to tears over some quite trivial mishap, he was well protected by his own determination to meet the crisis head-on. He worked – there was no other word for it – as hard as he knew how to repair and rebuild our marriage. He was helped too by his eagerness to know the truth: he had not been fooled by our story of my going away 'to think', for one evening he came into my room and made an astute guess as to the real reason for my 'row' with Mummy, which I confirmed. Only at nights did he weaken, kissing me with unusual fervour when I said my goodnight words to him, holding on to my neck and refusing to let me go. However, I knew he was on the way to recovering his equilibrium when, a week or so after my coming back, instead of lying quietly in his bed and waiting for my kiss, he greeted me cheerfully, saying, 'Have you heard this one, Dad?'

'No. Which one?'

'If a cow had a wooden tit, it would have a wooden tit, wouldn't it?'

I laughed and said his special words, to which he paid only perfunctory attention. He had evidently decided that things were getting back to normal.

Tilly, on the other hand, responded quite differently to my

departure and return. Like Jack, she welcomed me home with great joy, but thereafter she made no comment, and did not join in his reparative efforts. I could not believe that she had not been disturbed by my absence and the obvious suffering Sally had undergone, yet she showed no sign of it, remaining cool and apparently untouched for two days. Then, on the Tuesday following the Sunday of my return, she suddenly broke.

Wearing her uniform with her usual panache, and seeming to be in cheerful spirits, she went to her Brownies' meeting that evening, but when she got back she was crying for no reason that we could divine or she would explain. Nor could we console her, and she continued to cry during her bath and after she had been put to bed.

I went upstairs to see her.

'What's the matter?'

She shook her head.

'Is it X?' I mentioned the name of a girl at school, who had been making life difficult for her.

This time she shook her head more emphatically.

'Is it because you think I'm going to go away again?'

'Yes.' She began to cry violently and helplessly.

I spoke to her at great length, reassuring her that I was not going to leave, promising her that I never would. As I talked her crying gradually stopped and I saw her sink back on her pillow, visibly relaxing.

Her eyes wandered from mine, and she interrupted me.

'Where's my Snugglebum?' she asked. This referred to a repellent and much-loved creature of plastic and nylon fur, which she had been given for her birthday. I looked for it, without success, assuring her that I would look again the next morning, in the daylight. More than anything else, the fact that she was not upset by its temporary disappearance made me think that she was reassured.

I, however, was very worried by the incident. Apart from feeling acute remorse, I was shocked by her ability to conceal her thoughts and emotions so thoroughly. From now onwards, I knew we would never be certain what fears, doubts and confusions she was nursing. Jack's face and behaviour can be openly read, but hers turn out to be sealed and disguised. This is not a matter of her being older, it demonstrates a real difference between their personalities. They have both shown great courage and resourcefulness over these critical weeks, but by being so enigmatic her mode of coping is far harder to support.

Early this morning, before we were awake, it snowed. The children were thrilled and rushed outside to roll little snowballs out of the thin layer on our drive. The snow signals the end of the glorious autumn that has brought so much unhappiness, and signals the beginning of a winter that will be very hard for Sally and me.

Recently, the children have shown no overt signs of disturbance. Jack continues to be watchful; he has also developed a genially avuncular interest in our 'romantic' life, encouraging us to kiss and cuddle, and beaming roguishly at us when we do so. Tilly has not given way to crying again, but of course it is now difficult for us to tell with her what is restraint, and what is a genuine recovery of her *joie de vivre*. Since the events of three weeks ago, they have both been unusually pliable and biddable, displaying a touching desire to have the ordinary, day-to-day routine run smoothly. Yet, for all that, I cannot judge the toll our unhappiness is taking from them. Not that Sally and I argue or fight; on the contrary, our relationship is, from the outside, the side they see, calm and equable. Within, it is full of sadness and conflict, but I hope that if they are aware of the strain between us, they are also aware of the mutual effort we are making to dispel it. Together and separately, we are able to give the children the concern and interest on which they rely for their well-being, though I still cannot give them the time they deserve. But then, whatever my contribution, I have always felt guilty about that. I am, at the least, able to give them my love, which is once more flowing freely in their direction.

DECEMBER

A desolate, but insipid December has set in. Except for the fact the trees are bare and the temperature is a few degrees colder, winter is turning out to be indistinguishable from the grey, drenched summer we have just endured. As if to reflect the mood of this house, it has rained more or less continually since I returned from Norfolk. Although we have now stopped crying, the rain, showing no respect for pathetic fallacies, persists. Our short drive is a quagmire, the woods are impassably marshy, and everything droops, rots or falls into its own mire.

Tilly was conceived in the December of 1976. It seemed very important to us that our baby should be conceived deliberately and consciously, that the precise moment of creation should be known to us and experienced as such. Our hopes of conceiving subtly changed the quality of our love-making; the knowledge that life, if it grew, would have been sparked into being by a known gesture of love was profoundly satisfying to both of us. I wanted our creation to be perfect. The baby was to be a work of art, and every stage of its making had to be flawless and untainted. New beginnings have always possessed a strong magic for me. The idea of starting afresh, free from the past and its failings, has been an illusion on which I have more than once built a solid and enduring reality. Of all the opportunities in my life, having a baby with Sally seemed to offer the best promise of an immaculate conception!

As far as these things can be accurately calculated, we later worked out that the actual moment of Tilly's inception took place, suitably enough, in my parents' house, where we stayed that year the weekend before Christmas. Though our decision to have a child had been taken mutually and with equal commitment, I look in vain at my diary at the time for evidence of some new steadiness of character, some sense of having planted my feet more firmly in anticipation of my new role. It appears that my mind was, on the contrary, in a state of unsuitable turmoil. The nearest entry to the first day of Tilly's existence comprises earnest notes on Marx's *Economic and Philosophical Manuscripts* of 1844. This is followed incongruously by a description of a wrestling match I had seen in Bury St Edmunds, with Klondike Jim and the ravishing Mitzi Mueller on the bill. 'Appalled (and excited) by the violence. Will not go again.'

Another entry in my diary for that period reads, 'I want to write a story about a man who attempts to shed his old personality and adopt a completely new one.' Some time later I did write this story in the form of a short thriller. As if taking dictation, I typed it out with exhilarating speed and ease, never hesitating from day to day, and within three months it was done. It was the fastest book I had ever written, and the worst. Despite knowing its inadequacy, I submitted it to publisher after publisher, and it was not until I had accumulated a dozen rejections that I at last surrendered.

My forlorn persistence was partly due to obstinacy, but more to the hold this fantasy of redemption and renewal had over me. It was a perennial idea of mine that it was possible to assume an entirely fresh identity, to remake the personality by ditching old faults and adopting new virtues. An essential feature of the fantasy was that the first, primitive self should pupate, like a caterpillar, in order to turn itself into the resplendent butterfly of the second self. For the purposes of my novel, I had to arrange for the hero to suffer an apparently fatal accident, involving the disappearance of his body, which would thus leave him free to prepare for his superior existence. With what I thought of at the time as marvellous ingenuity, I had him fake his own death by leaving unmistakable evidence of having fallen over one of Stackpole's fearsome cliffs. Once his absence had been noticed, his distraught family were to discover his last, slithering footprint and – a poignant touch this – his umbrella, abandoned as he tumbled off the edge. The credulous police would assume that his corpse had been sucked on to the rocks and pulverized to an unsalvageable pulp. Shaving off his beard with an electric razor, my hero meanwhile proceeded to catch a bus to his new life, which in fact he was never to enjoy. I lacked the conviction to see my fantasy through, and instead of allowing him to live out his glorious destiny, I had him go homicidally mad.

What I did not realize as I schemed this conspiracy on behalf of my futile hero was that I myself was undergoing a true metamorphosis, quite as wonderful as any butterfly's, in being turned into a father. This is a form of existence which is not only a kind of rebirth, but one that carries absolute credibility, at least in the eyes of those to whom it is most important. Children, after all, have no preconceived notion of how their fathers, or mothers, should be, and will happily accept any version of the role, however eccentric, providing their needs are adequately met.

I cannot recall that either of us looked to a particular model on which to base ourselves as parents. Obviously, everyone's idea of being a parent is affected, consciously or otherwise, by his or her own childhood experience, but at that stage, when pregnancy was no more than a hopeful possibility, we were thoughtless and carefree, happy to let nature determine our new identities. Our decision to have children had been made, in principle, almost as soon as we met. I had felt for a long time that not to have children was to remain unfulfilled, unfinished, only half-alive. This notion was, however, strictly abstract, because, as I said before, my experience of real children was negligible. 'Producing a child', I wrote solemnly, 'is both the greatest act of self-aggrandizement and self-effacement.' I did not know what I was talking about. For Sally, the situation was nearly the same: although she knew more parents with small children than I, she still had no real idea of what it was to be entirely responsible for a baby. And so, in this state of happy ignorance and, on my side, lofty pretentiousness, we set about the creation of a new life. Looking back, however, I can think of no better frame of mind in which to launch a first pregnancy.

In the November of that year my house in London was finally sold, yielding me the then staggering sum of £7000, which was enough for us to live on for the next year at least, and this precipitated our decision to take Sally off the pill. The last link with my old London life was snapped, and I felt an unexpected sense of liberation. The cheque came through at the end of the month, an event which we celebrated the same day with the purchase of a revolving bookcase and a vast, Baroque sofa, in keeping with the grandeur of our plans for the future.

Sally became pregnant at the next biologically possible moment.

Three Decembers later, in 1979, our lives were very different. Tilly had just turned two, and Jack was less than a year old, on the brink of walking. For eighteen months of those two years Sally had been pregnant, and for two of them we had not had an uninterrupted night's sleep; nor were we to enjoy this luxury for the next two years.

My diaries of that period read rather like the log book of a submarine captain: I seem to be reporting on the activities and relationships of a small crew doomed to an interminable voyage beneath the waves. We were at war with an enemy that was nameless, unseen and far above us – survival, in a word – but the real war was between ourselves, forced on us by the pressure of confinement in our cramped, airless capsule.

As in wartime, fatigue was the true enemy. During one particular week, Tilly was sick either in her bed or ours on five successive nights; Jack, meanwhile, was extremely restless, never waking less than half a dozen times during the course of a night, and requiring prolonged attention before going back to sleep. In trying to soothe him, I would stand in the dark, hold him tightly to my chest and rock him to and fro. In time, his breathing would slow, his body would slacken and fall inert, and I would relax my grasp. Taking my pace from him, I would slow my rocking until I was convinced he was fully immersed in sleep. Then, moving with imperceptible steps, I would ease myself towards his bed and begin the laborious process of depositing him on to the pillow. Inch by inch, my back cracking with pain, I would bend lower and lower, hovering for a moment between each little stage of the descent. Seemingly fast asleep, he would allow me to get within a hair's breadth of the sheet. However, the instant we made contact, he would wake and cry, whereupon the whole ritual would have to begin again.

It was not even possible to sit down and rock him. Standing up, I would put him to sleep and position myself above a chair. Then, exercising the kind of muscular control an Olympic gymnast would be proud of, I would gradually bend my knees, while still maintaining the rhythm of his rocking, but just as I was about to slide through the final millimetre of agonized declension, he would stir and yell his protest.

As often as not, we would be driven to take first one and then the other into our bed, where they at least would finally rest. It was always a wonderful relief to feel their crying subside, to hear their breathing decelerate and deepen, and, in Jack's case, to hear it swell into a thunderous snore. We, however, could never sleep for long. Although at that age children are delightful companions in bed, in that they want nothing so much as to exchange the closest physical affection, they are also very disturbing. Tilly and Jack were ceaselessly on the move when asleep; indeed, they were hardly less active than when awake. They flung out their arms, stretched expansively, rolled, writhed, twitched and moaned, and usually contrived to lie laterally, sometimes across our faces. With the four of us together, this had the effect of forcing Sally and me to our respective edges, to which we clung desperately, like climbers on a rock face. Not content with pushing us off the bed, they used to kick as well. I would often feel a small foot searching for my back, which, once located, would receive a smart blow. After such a night, we would wake, if we had been lucky enough to fall asleep, feeling not only jaded, but bruised too.

During this period, Jack was going through a phase of late-night activity, which Tilly had only just grown out of. As we lay in bed, blearily staring at our books for a minute or two before putting out the light, he would wake and, instead of crying, would call out in the most sociable tone. Fearing that he would wake Tilly, we would have to bring him into our room and let him play on the bed, where we would be treated to his entire repertoire of jokes and tricks. Since he had not yet learnt to talk, these mostly consisted of his hiding his face and laughing uproariously each time he uncovered it. This entertainment called for very little response on our part, but would continue in its relentlessly genial way for half an hour or more. Yet, in spite of our exhaustion, it seemed wrong to stop him and crush his innocent merriment. We would doze at one end of the bed, while he chortled and burrowed at the other, until at last he would fall silent. Apart from knowing that he would not have gone back to his bed before, we were also conscious, in our doziness, that these ill-timed sessions were somehow very important to his development. With Tilly asleep, this was one of the few times when he enjoyed our undivided, if glazed, attention, and he seemed to grow up almost visibly as he entertained us with his one-man cabarets.

This chronic fatigue took its toll, especially of Sally, and was probably much more destructive than we realized. The constant vigilance required in looking after small children drains the mind as much as the body of its energy. While the children are awake, there is no relief, because even during the rare moments when they do not need to be picked up, moved, rescued, comforted, restrained or manhandled in some other way, they are still a responsibility, which allows no respite. Your eye is forever flickering anxiously in their direction; your thoughts are always tinged with worry; all your instincts are sharpened on their behalf; and your ability to concentrate on anything else for longer than a few seconds is simply suspended.

Sally and I were pale and haggard, we walked in slow motion, and we yawned continuously. Our landscape was a grey Arctic of nappies: stinking nappies left to soak in buckets, nappies abandoned during a crisis and left to suppurate in some forgotten corner, nappies in the wash, on the line, and draped over the Aga to dry in a hurry, nappies drooping down the children's legs, and nappies on the kitchen table, folded in readiness for the next change. Pinning clean nappies on a wriggling and resistant baby ten times a day is tiring enough in itself, but nothing is more dispiriting or wearisome than having sewage disposal forced on you as a permanent way of life.

If the children went to bed during the day, or were taken out by the other, Sally and I would fall asleep instantly. Sally did so openly, usually at the kitchen table, her head on her arms. I slept covertly, in my room, under the pretext of working. At the time, I was having to read a great deal to research a book of my own, but it proved to be the book which took me the longest to write and was the shortest in words. I could not work for sleeping. I knew that if I were to sit in my armchair, my eyes would be shut before they had plodded across a line of type. The only way I could keep going was by confining myself to the hard, upright chair at my desk, but even then I would drop dormantly over the typewriter, telling myself I needed to rest my eyes for a moment. And then the house would fall quite silent.

Our exhaustion brought a terrible tension to the business of getting the children to bed at nights. So much seemed to be at stake. We felt that if we did not get the evenings to ourselves, we would forfeit the chance of recovering our old identities. Not that we ever did much with these child-free interludes except drowse over the television, but we did relish the sensation of being people in our own right, of filling some role other than those of minder, dresser, play leader, lavatory attendant and so on. Putting the children to sleep came to mean more than winning a few hours' peace and relaxation, though that was crucial too. It involved the positive suppression of their existence in order that ours could continue. We felt that without this brief, nightly abeyance of ourselves as parents, without this little restitution of our old being, we would be lost, helplessly submerged beneath the children's demands and needs. Their survival depended on us, a responsibility that we had got badly out of proportion, but in its turn our survival seemed to depend on these intervals of their non-existence. To this day, I attach a quite unnecessary urgency to putting them to bed: I still feel that some vital part of myself will be repressed if they do not withdraw promptly at the end of the day.

For the last ten days Jack has spent every available hour digging a hole. The site of his excavation is immediately outside my window, so I have been able to observe its progress closely. Standing opposite my side of the house and just beside the barn the children use as a playroom is a Scots pine, which leans at a precarious angle, and it was at the foot of our Pisan tree that Jack and a schoolfriend began to dig one afternoon. In its youth the tree was the victim, so we were told, of a near-fatal blow struck by a careless tank, but it survived and went on to grow as it had been left, at forty-five degrees. It would have fallen down long since under its own weight, had not the branches on its lower side been cut away so that a large limb on the other side could act as a counterbalance to the trunk. As a result, it thrives on the thin, sandy soil in that part of the garden, which even our resident mole disdains.

Darkness fell and the sappers were still digging. Finally, Jack's muddy face loomed out of the night.

'Look, Dad,' he shouted through my window. 'Coal!'

He held up a crumbly black stone.

This lone nugget proved to be the limit of their success as miners, but neither darkness nor hunger halted their operations. They ate their sandwiches underground, and pressed on by candlelight.

The same indefatigable team reassembled the next afternoon, and Jack continued to dig, with and without help, throughout the rest of the week. His hole grew wide enough to accommodate two small boys wielding shovels, and deep enough to conceal all but their bobbing heads. The sheer hard work he brought to his task was impressive, but there was something manic about it as well. It is true that children never do anything in a desultory, half-hearted fashion, yet his devotion to his hole was more than energetic. It became an obsession with him, and no one who came to the house could avoid being dragged out to inspect and admire his labours.

For a while I thought his compulsive tunnelling might have a sexual meaning, but then it occurred to me that he might be trying to dig himself *out*, that he was tunnelling to escape from our present situation. He certainly persists with his campaign to strengthen our reunion. Only yesterday he brought me a matchbox wrapped in Christmas paper; it was empty, but presented with great ceremony, and I could only assume that he intended it as a bribe to keep me here. Although he no longer talks about his fears of my leaving again, I believe they still haunt him. Both he and Tilly always ask with uncharacteristic urgency when I will be coming back if ever I go away for the day. They demand to know the exact time of my return and are visibly reassured when they are told.

I decided to test my theory and ask him about his hole.

'Are you digging to Australia?' I asked him, standing at the brink of his pit.

'Naaah,' he said, sarcastically. 'What do I want to go there for?'

'Are you digging for coal?'

'No. There's no treasures here.'

He pointed glumly to a little pile of uninteresting flints and stones he had unearthed.

'Are you trying to dig yourself out of something?'

He looked at me, evidently stupefied by the silliness of my question.

'I'm digging,' he said, speaking slowly, as if to a moron, 'to make the hole bigger.'

This was unanswerable, so I left him to it.

The period when the children were very small and absolutely dependent on us probably did more damage to Sally than me, though its long-term effects are turning out to be more decisive in my case than hers. Sally's sense of her own self took a cruel battering. She had expected to be a 'natural mother', but was shocked to discover that her material resources were far from limitless, and that caring for the children did not come to her either effortlessly or spontaneously. As well as being exhausted, she was tormented with anxiety: the children's very lives were in her hands and she did not feel equal to the task. Furthermore, her identity seemed to have been rubbed out by motherhood, not enhanced. She only knew who she was as a mother, but her idea of herself as a woman, wife, lover, friend and businesswoman had been shattered. Not surprisingly, these feelings of self-effacement sometimes ignited outbursts of awful rage and violence, especially at nights when she resented my not taking an equal share in getting up to the children when they woke. I of course resented her unjust accusation, as I saw it, and so the fatigue of arguing was added to the sum of our other fatigues.

However, these things are never simple. Looking back on our somnambulist days, I can see now they were also a period when, if we were not exactly happy, we were deeply fulfilled. But then what is happiness, if it is not a sense of fulfilment? No matter how arduous the job, we knew just what we were supposed to be doing. Whether we chafed against it or not, our role was unmistakably defined: when the children cried, we ran to their comfort; when they were hungry, we fed them; when they got dirty, we cleaned them up; when they smiled, we smiled back. All our activities were in some way determined by the children, who also laid down the terms of our relationship. They demanded nothing less than total engagement with us, and that is what we gave them. We became utterly absorbed in the children, as they were in us. And, despite our misgivings, we were manifestly succeeding. Far from dying, the children thrived. They grew bigger, they learnt to talk and walk, they stopped crying and began to make their needs felt in much more amusing ways. Although their power over us seemed, if anything, to strengthen, their dictatorship became more benign. The children were never out of my thoughts, but because I was able to go to my room and pursue my work, albeit somnolently, I did perhaps find it easier than Sally to enjoy the satisfactions and rewards of being a parent. I could reflect on them in relative tranquillity, while she was seldom free to do so. Yet, for all that, Sally and I had never been closer: we were a team, indissolubly united in our devotion to this common task. *A Father's Diary* is both a product of, and a tribute to, that era of total family involvement, when there was never a dull or empty day, never a day without achievement.

Thus, we were in the grip of two very powerful, but contrary emotions: we both felt our identities crumbling under the onslaught of children, and yet neither of us had previously known the same absolute certainty regarding our roles in life. And in both cases, this conflict has only recently begun to work itself out. When the children finally went to school, acquiring a social life of their own, as well as a new and disconcerting independence of mind, we were liberated from the old regime that had ruled us for more than seven years; yet we also suffered a loss. We were free, but we were redundant too. However, while some changes occur catastrophically, and their effects cannot fail to be felt, others come about slowly and insidiously, their effects remaining invisible and unrecognized long after the event. We rejoiced in our new-found liberty, but I don't think either of us realized until much later that we had been cast adrift, on dangerous waters, and, to keep up the metaphor, in separate boats. We were no longer bound to the children, but in being released from them, we both set out to rediscover ourselves, to confirm our attractiveness, and to impinge on the world outside as individuals not parents.

Sally's reaction to her freedom was, oddly enough, to engage in yet another maternal activity. She decided to keep sheep. As the children required less and less of her time, she built up her flock, committing herself to her new family quite as intensely as she had to her old one. By this year's spring she and her partner had made themselves responsible for no less than one hundred and fifty animals – fifty ewes and their assorted lambs. This proved too much even for her formidable energies. Her partnership is now over and the flock sold, leaving a small, manageable nucleus of ten experienced matrons, who will enjoy the luxurious facilities of our garage when this spring's lambing comes round. What Sally will put her energy into next is not certain, but I do not believe she will allow it to take her as far away from the children and me again.

On reflection, I think I found the emptiness brought about by the children's departure to school harder to cope with than Sally, though I did not know it at the time. By being at home all day while the children were small, I became more of a mother than a father to them; or perhaps it would be fairer to say I became their assistant mother. In any event, when the family began to disperse, and Sally and I were no longer harnessed together as a team, I did not have a clear conception of what I wanted to become. My identity, my sense of who I was, had always been confused, but now I knew neither what sort of parent I was to be, nor what sort of man. The tragedy was, however, that as the children made their necessary and healthy withdrawal from the nest, I too withdrew, not only from them, but from Sally as well, leaving the family with a hollow centre.

In a child's calendar no month, even the holiday month of August, is more significant than December. Now that the children are both at school, their Christmas hysteria does not become seriously frenzied until the last two weeks before the great day. When they were smaller, however, they used to run the gamut from starry-eyed anticipation to bilious disgust before November was out. In those days, it was impossible to protect them from the intoxications of shop windows and the heaps of decorated things inside, all of which registered in their fevered minds as toys, and their excitement would rapidly sour into frustration. Far from being a period of magical expectation, December became a term of torment, though Christmas Day itself never lost its sublime thrill.

This year, because they have hardly been to Bury St Edmunds, they have remained more or less calm until we put up our tree in the kitchen last Saturday. Each afternoon since then on their return from school they have rushed directly to the pile of parcels gathering under its branches to count the new ones bearing their names. These they lovingly turn over and over, squeezing and shaking them, feeling their weight, and trying to guess from their size and shape what they contain. Finally, they subside in quiet ecstasy on to the floor to fondle them. Their belief in Father Christmas, incidentally, undergoes a wonderful resurgence with the approach of the twenty-fifth. Throughout the rest of the year they sneer cynically at the mention of his name, as befits their grand maturity, but when they think disbelief might put at risk the number of their presents they become droolingly credulous.

For me, as a small boy, Christmas meant going to my

Stackpole grandparents. We went there every year of my childhood, and I don't suppose the rituals varied much, if at all, yet I have only the most scattered memories of all those Christmases. Having no older siblings to throw doubt on my faith, I believed – fervently – in Father Christmas for far longer than my children did. I was told that he visited our house not via the traditional chimney, but, more decorously, through the French windows into the sitting room. Why this was, I cannot remember, though I do recall taking a snobbish pride in the fact that he favoured my family with this unusual means of entry. A glass of sherry and mince pies were left out for him on a little table by the window, and I was put to bed.

My room, which formed a corner of the house, seemed to me enormous, and my double bed was in keeping with its gigantic proportions. At night, alone in the dark, I felt as if I were drifting in an open boat, surrounded by a black and fathomless sea. The distant wall opposite, lit up by a seam of light above the door, was like a cliff, whose foot was lapped by the liquid carpet, and whose surface was pitted with the shadowy caves of alcoves and a great booming fireplace. Hanging above it was a pair of fairy pictures, whose wings were made from real butterflies, and in the half-dark they glittered like phosphorescent flying fish. All children experience these moments of nocturnal loneliness with a special and never-repeated intensity, but I believe only children, having no one to share them with, no one to call out to, experience them with extra horror. Certainly, I was too frightened to put a foot overboard for fear of sinking in the waves.

My bed was equipped with an old-fashioned, solid bolster, which ran the width of the bedhead and acted as a kind of gunwale, protecting me from the predatory swell. It failed me only once. I woke one night to find myself trapped beneath the blankets. I tunnelled towards the surface, but could not find an opening. I seemed to have been sewn into the bed, and like a kitten drowning in a bag, the harder I struggled the more I suffocated. In fact, my bolster had somehow blocked off my escape, but not knowing it, I turned round and began to thrash towards the bottom of the bed. Of course, I found my way out in the end, but to this day I cannot read of a death at sea without remembering the terror of my own dry drowning.

In order that I should not wake the household on Christmas morning, it was arranged with Father Christmas that he would deposit my presents in the bathroom, a room which, perhaps for this reason, I recall with rare clarity. It had a large, coiled, shiny towel rail, presumably heated by the Aga from the kitchen below, and was always warm. Its bath was impressive for being much bigger than ours at home, and when its green, perished-rubber plug was pulled the water ran out with a distinctive, bronchial gurgle, which I have never heard reproduced by any other bath. The rule was that I had to stay in bed until it was light outside; then I was allowed to run to the bathroom and open my presents, which were hung over the back of a rocking chair. Although I can remember the chill of the corridor and the exhilarating sensation of bursting into the warmth of the bathroom to find that glowing heap of parcels, I cannot remember a single one of the hundreds of presents I must have received over all those years. Not one of those toys, which were so carefully chosen and wrapped, so laboriously transported down from Liverpool, ripped so frantically from their paper, and which were presumably cherished and played with for weeks after, not one of them has lodged in my memory.

The only memory I have, which is associated with a specific Christmas Day toy, is of a walk with my father down to Broadhaven beach. I cannot date the year, but there was snow on the sand and a brown ice had formed on the surface of the lily pond, locking the windblown froth into a sort of chocolate ice-cream. This walk was made thrilling to me because I was able to flourish a new weapon at the innumerable enemies which stalked us behind every sand dune. My father was very imaginative when we came to play such games, and he slaughtered quite as many savages as I did, despatching them with splendid panache. But exactly what my new weapon was, whether a rifle, pistol, bow and arrow, or knife, I cannot recall, try as I might.

My grandfather died in 1962 on Boxing Day, just as the snow was beginning to fall. By then we were no longer spending our summer holidays at Stackpole, but the Christmas tradition had been maintained. I was eighteen and had left school only a week before, at the end of that winter term, with a university place waiting for me in the following September. The months to come stretched ahead of me, their emptiness haunted by the grim spectre of having to take some kind of job, a misfortune I had so far managed to evade.

Of the circumstances of my grandfather's death and preceding illness, I remember nothing; but by that time he had ceased to be the fearsome figure of my childhood, and had become an old man, whose authority no longer impinged on me. I had of course grown older myself, but I can pinpoint the moment when I struck off the manacles of his scorn. A year or so before he died, my mother, he and I were driving somewhere in our car and the subject of Roman Catholicism came up for discussion. My grandfather made a pronouncement, which he evidently regarded as definitive, but which, to his surprise, I challenged in a lengthy speech rendered all the more remarkable by my complete ignorance of Catholic theology. My windy disquisition brought the debate to a halt and, after an astonished silence, he said, 'Well. You're not such a fool then!'

I was pleased by my triumph, but it was also my turn to be astonished, for I remember thinking, 'Is that all? Is that what it's been about all these years?'

I knew that what I had been saying was blithering nonsense wrapped up in a few fancy phrases and uttered in a know-all tone (I had, after all, passed divinity 'O' level), but he was too unsophisticated to see through my flannel. For seventeen years I had been condemned as a fool by someone who could be so easily deceived by what really was a piece of foolishness. I had not been a fool as a child, I had merely been vulnerable, but now I was strong enough to stand up to him with my new-found pretentiousness, the silly old man was impressed.

He died suddenly of his third heart attack. He was seventy-three and had enjoyed a much longer life than had been predicted for him when he suffered his first, nearly fatal attack thirteen years earlier. Those days before the funeral were miserable ones for my mother, who not only had to cope with her grief, but also had to look after the gathering ranks of our relatives. Forgotten aunts and remote cousins battled through the weather to join us, hotel rooms were booked, extra beds were made up, huge quantities of food were prepared, terrible decisions were taken and the house began to be dismantled. I, however, took no part in any of these melancholy rites. Wonderfully insulated by adolescent selfishness, I kept out of the way and read books or mooned about the farm, as I had always done. I was sorry for my mother, but felt no grief of my own.

My grandfather was buried in Stackpole churchyard next to my grandmother, who had died four years earlier. That winter was one of the most severe in living memory and the sextons must have had a hard job digging his grave. A path had been cut from the church to the graveside, but as the mourners filed from the porch to attend the burial, snow began to fall again, and the long black ribbon of coats, hats and umbrellas was gradually turned white. I had never looked into an open grave before, and I was shocked by its depth. My handful of earth and snow took far longer than I expected to drop down and rattle on the lid of his coffin.

*

Last night, the first truly hard frost of the winter struck, and no matter how much fuel we heaped on to our wood-burner we could not get warm. The sky was clear, with a fine crop of stars, the moon was full, and the grass at my feet, as I took a swift midnight stroll, was ice-crisp and sparkling with rime. This afternoon, the ground is still granite-hard, as if it had been paved, and the water in the pot-holes outside my window is frozen to the bottom. A dim-witted blackbird persists in trying to bathe, going through all its habitual motions, fluttering open its wing feathers, dipping its legs and flicking the immovable water with its beak. It has bathed in the same spot for weeks and will not accept that the facility is now shut for the duration. The extreme hardness of the earth has forced our mole almost to the surface. Earlier, when I was on the telephone and helpless to use the opportunity, I saw it forging through the lawn, humping up the grass in a chain of mole-sized long barrows.

On the field opposite our house, pheasants are making a Christmas feast on the sugar beet tops and fattening themselves unwittingly for the last drives of the season. They have been joined by numberless hordes of pigeons, which rise at the slightest alarm in solid clouds and scatter in a sky the colour of their plumage, before wheeling and settling once more on the unprotected ground. The only real colour to be seen is in the red stripes of the partridges' waistcoats and the dazzling cobalt flashes on the wings of jays, which gather along our drive to pick berries and acorns. The children, usually impervious to cold, have been driven indoors and the birds have the garden to themselves. A blue-tit with a long memory has been tapping all afternoon at my window where I hung a bird feeder last year. A robin seems to have made the hedges outside our front door the headquarters of its territory, and a kestrel, which usually hunts the far end of the drive, is hovering above the house, perhaps watching for the field mice that take refuge in our barn during the worst of the cold.

Christmas is over now, and thanks largely to the generosity and unfailing good spirits of Sally's parents, we have all thoroughly enjoyed ourselves. The dustbin is full of torn wrapping paper and empty bottles. Toys, discarded as soon as they were ripped from their parcels, litter the bedrooms. The fridge is a charnel house of poultry bones, the television is red-hot from continual use, and the sitting room reeks of stale cigar smoke. Though they may not sound it, these are sure signs of pleasure, for we did all these things together, children and grandparents binding together the fracture in our marriage, which is beginning to set.

November still overshadows everything Sally and I do or think, but the children seem to be creeping slowly from beneath its darkness. Christmas has restored our sense of being a family, and the children show some confidence in our reunion; it will, however, take Sally far longer to do the same. I know it to be true, but no amount of telling will yet convince her that I could never again leave her and the children. I still do not properly understand what drove me away; perhaps I never will. Sally asks for explanations all the time; the children ask for none. The children are right, for in the end only time will reassure her, but she is entitled to hear an account of my actions that make them intelligible. How else is she to rebuild her self-esteem? How else am I to be forgiven?

Whatever the difficulties between Sally and myself, how could I ever have contemplated leaving the children? This is the question most often asked. I now look back on my desertion of them as an interlude of madness, which I find almost impossible to analyse. Confusion and turmoil are all I see when I look back. I had lost my way very badly. To be a parent calls for a measure of certainty regarding who you are, who you wish your children to become and how you believe they should be brought up. During the summer of 1985 I discovered, to my horror, I knew none of these things. When the children were babies, their needs more or less determined our way of life and defined our identity, but as they became schoolchildren I stumbled into a void. I still needed them to give shape and meaning to my life, but now they needed me in ways I could not satisfy. I had surprised myself, and probably everyone else, by being a proficient and patient mother-father, but when it came to being a parent of children who had outgrown nappies and required a more sophisticated level of help and education, I felt I was failing them. The more they asked of me – and they asked for nothing out of the ordinary – the more conscious I became of my inadequacy. I did not seem to be able to teach them anything, to illuminate the world for them, or equip them with any cast-iron values. I could not recognize that what I had been giving them in the way of ordinary, day-to-day affection and fun would still have been sufficient. I had a far more grandiose idea of myself as a parent; yet it was one I could not fulfil, and did not meet my children's real wants.

I had just turned forty, I had tasted a little professional success, which, paradoxically, can be most disturbing, I had not settled into our new house, and I was boiling with a volatile, highly explosive energy, which I could neither disperse nor subdue. All this, but especially the belief that I was failing as a parent, drove the wedge between the children and myself. I loved them – I loved them intensely – yet I could not devote my love directly and immediately to them. It was obstructed by these confusions and feelings, which now seem to add up to so much folly, but at the time possessed the hideous, inescapable reality of a nightmare.

However wrong I was in my method of doing it, I was perhaps right to force things to a climax. The only way of arresting this racing chaos was to overwhelm it with some catastrophe, just as forest fires are sometimes halted by massive explosions detonated in their path. I did indeed bring down catastrophe on us, but while I deeply regret the pain I caused Sally, I know that I would have caused her still more suffering had I not done what I did. At least I have now replaced confusion with certainty: I know I want to be here, and that I will never leave. That terrible frenzied energy, which threatened to tear everything apart, has been converted back into passion – for the children, and for Sally.

We will endure; of that I am certain.

JANUARY

We spent New Year's Eve at Peter's cottage in Stowlangtoft. The children went upstairs to Sylvia's room to play Monopoly, and we forgot about them, imagining they had fallen asleep. However, when I went up to look at them around ten o'clock, I found the game still in full swing. The girls had ruthlessly ground Jack into the gutter, making him sell his properties at knock-down prices to raise a few last despairing pounds, which they promptly took off him in rent. He was staring at the board, a shattered man.

'I've lost all my money,' he repeated tonelessly, not even looking up at me.

'That's the game,' crowed the girls in chorus, as they prepared yet another ruinous mortgage for him.

'I've nothing left,' he moaned, and appeared to be on the point of leaping from the window.

Just before midnight I went up again and this time found him actually standing at the window, but it was a misunderstanding, not suicidal despondency, that had brought him there. Having heard us talk about 'seeing in' the New Year, he thought, reasonably enough, that it was a phenomenon you could observe, like Halley's comet or the new moon. By now their faces were ghostly with exhaustion, but they came downstairs to clink glasses with us and shout 'Happy New Year' with rousing gusto. Though the New Year means far less to them than Christmas or birthdays, they love ceremony and ritual for their own sake.

At the beginning of each year, I look back and try to assess how the children have changed over the previous twelve months. This is always a surprisingly difficult exercise, because they do not evolve smoothly along a steady incline of maturation; instead, they grow up by means of sudden, sporadic leaps, acquiring skills overnight which the day before were utterly beyond them and for which they seem to need no practice.

During the last year, Jack has lost his old thirst for mayhem and murder, though his games still have a distinctly militaristic flavour. Whenever he makes a camp or sets out on one of his expeditions, he is sure to be heavily armed and thoroughly equipped, as if for an arduous campaign, but his generally homicidal manner has declined. The punch is no longer his customary mode of greeting, and he no longer feels the need to saw off your leg or shoot you full of holes in order to convey his affection. He has not only lost his old pugnacity, but has become subdued, and even a little obsequious. A year or so ago, when he entered a room he would discombobulate it, to borrow a splendid American word from the late Orson Welles, who used it to describe his own turbulent impact on a film set. But nowadays he is anxious to please and still bends all his efforts to ensuring that harmony reigns between Sally and myself.

The other day he announced he was going to call a meeting, which he expected the whole family to attend. The only item on his agenda turned out to be the banning of rows among us. I thought this was an admirable proposal, showing his usual concern for our well-being, though I was sorry he still had the impression we were at odds. Sally and I continue to have our moments of conflict and unhappiness, but we have made a pact to display a united front in the children's presence and until he called his meeting I believed we were beginning to reassure them. Evidently, their powers of discernment are sharper than we supposed. I was much more concerned, however, by another remark he made on the same occasion.

'I'm going to live on my own when I grow up,' he informed Sally, 'and I'm not going to have any children.'

By this I understood him to mean that he had got round to think that our difficulties were his fault, that he was somehow responsible for my leaving. I have read that this misplaced guilt often afflicts the children of divorcing couples. In his case, it is very sad he is unable to realize that, far from being the cause of any rift between us, his attempts to reunite us have indeed brought us closer, and have played a significant part in making us determined to hold our marriage together. Tilly's attempts to mend our breach are subtler than his, less overt, but no less moving. Throughout, she has maintained both her courage and her dignity, and I know I have drawn on her steadiness. Without saying much, she has shown us by her behaviour that she trusts us to put things right and restore the old world. In supporting us they are of course protecting their own interests, but in their different ways they have done so with a generosity that belies their years.

I must not give the impression that Jack's spirit has been broken. He is still very capable of roaring round the house, laughing fiendishly at jokes beyond adult comprehension and playing tricks on anyone unfortunate enough to offer himself as a victim, but he is nevertheless more submissive, or perhaps more serious, than he was a year ago. Tilly, on the other hand, has grown more rumbustious and much more self-confident. She has also become galvanized by some form of energy, which renders her perpetually mobile. To have Jack on your knee is to be soothed and warmed by a boy-shaped hot water bottle; to have Tilly on your knee is to enjoy the doubtful pleasures of a waterless Jacuzzi, for she buffets you on every side with her wriggling. She is never at rest: her means of locomotion is an agitated mix of hopping, twirling, skipping and straight-forward crashing. She is not so much clumsy as dynamic. She affects the physical world like a poltergeist: pictures mysteriously fall to the floor as she passes, glasses spontaneously upend themselves and spray their contents, chairs slip their moorings and career across the floor; in short, she subverts the laws of gravity by her mere presence. And this bodily turmoil is matched by mental extremism. She exists in an atmosphere of high drama: nothing that is done to her is less than an outrage, eligible for the Court of Human Rights, nothing she achieves is less than a masterpiece, and nothing she puts her mind to is executed with less than daunting thoroughness. Her talents, whatever they prove to be, will never be underexploited, just as her faults will never be modest ones.

I can always write more easily about Jack than her, perhaps because he is a boy and I instinctively identify with his behaviour. However, there is a delicate subtlety to Tilly, combined with a tough self-sufficiency which he lacks, that makes her much harder to capture in simple, vivid strokes. Although many of our feelings for the children are undiscriminating – what we feel for one, we feel for both – there are of course some distinctions. Tilly was our first baby, and to the first-born a unique feeling will always be attached. I have learnt an enormous amount from both of them, but from Tilly we learnt what it was to be a parent, and in fact how to be a parent, for there is no other way of learning.

For some reason, which neither of us could explain, when Sally first became pregnant we both wanted a girl – in my case, passionately so. In this respect, and every other, Tilly fulfilled my parental fantasies. She was faultless in my eyes. I idealized her from the first moment of her life, and if her small feet were to harden into clay, I would never notice (or admit) it. I was fascinated, and bewitched, by this pretty being, who had achieved her coup d'état of our household simply by taking up residence. The older she grew, the more enslaved I became: no one had ever found my company as entertaining as she did, and the discovery was mutual. No one had ever thought me so useful, knowledgeable, practical or hilarious.

I remember her with special clarity as she was when Sally was pregnant with Jack, and she was just old enough to walk. Although unable to talk with any coherence, by her second January she was very capable of making her wishes clear. This she did with the aid of a whole language of gestures, expressions and noises, which she supplemented by the word 'down', an instruction drawn from our futile attempts to train our dogs. 'Down' became a command she put to universal use.

'Down! Down! Piggy!' she would shout at me, pointing eloquently at the door and making frantic up-and-down movements with her other hand. Then she would totter to the back door and begin the laborious business of pulling on her wellingtons and coat, whose zip she could not manage unassisted – hence her up-and-down motions. These signals would tell me that I was inescapably destined for our morning – or afternoon – trip across the farmyard to the pig houses.

Looking at the current Tilly, whose legs are attaining coltish grace and length, it is difficult to recall that she was in those days more or less spherical, especially when encased in her coat, which gave her the look of a doughnut on the run. She was also so small we could not hold hands on our expeditions unless I bent over and held her arm rigidly straight above her head. This had the advantage that if ever she tripped over or was in danger of wandering into a puddle, I only had to square my shoulders to hoist her into the air and hold her dangling above the ground.

First, we would visit the farrowing house, but despite the alarming resemblance of the pink and hairless piglets to human infants, she much preferred seeing the weaners in the fattening pens, which we visited next. Here, in the dust-laden half-dark, I would swing her up to sit on the wall and study the antics of the thirty or so piglings in the straw below. The slightest noise or movement would send them scurrying in panic to the far end of the pen, where they would bury themselves in a great squirming mass, snouts first, leaving their ridiculous tails exposed. Being inveterately curious and, no doubt, exceedingly bored, they would soon regain their confidence, and come skittering back to peer up at us, their knowing humanoid eyes apparently registering amusement. This invariable cycle gave Tilly much entertainment and she soon learnt to wait for them to relax before waving her arms and shouting. We could never leave the pens without her begging to scatter them one last time.

'More down, Daddy!' she would yell at me, meaning the opposite, as I tore her off the wall, her coat by now white with pig meal.

These experiences are unforgettable, particularly since, in my case, they were new. Before having my own children, I had never held a small child's hand, at least not for more than a moment. With Tilly, everything was new, and magical. From her we learnt the carefree sensuality that all small children radiate and indulge in; from her we learnt that there is no appropriate moment in the day for jokes, games, songs – and fights – for any moment will do; and she taught us the importance of dignity in small things, the need to leave other people the room and freedom to have their own being, however eccentric it might appear. To someone like myself, whose life had hitherto been grossly overstructured, these were not just important lessons, they were revelations.

Tilly will never lose that magic. She is of course more serious now, and she has become very quick – she is quick to learn, she has a quick tongue and wit, she moves quickly, and her moods are quick to change. She still bewitches me, and these days I am a little in awe of her. I only hope she is not too quick to judge, for I think I am still on trial in her mind.

In our family, one of the best-kept Yuletide traditions is that we are all ill. I cannot think of a Christmas holiday since the children were born when we have not been laid low by some virus. This year Tilly signalled the start of our regrettable custom by being sick in the middle of the night, though she was kind enough to do it in someone else's house. She was brought home in the morning and went to bed for the rest of the day, waking with the instinct of a true television addict seconds before the first episode of *Alice in Wonderland* was broadcast. Jack, meanwhile, had developed a tragic, hollow cough of the kind actors break their tonsils to produce in an effort to suggest the ravages of consumption. Sally lost her speaking, but not her shouting voice, and I felt as if someone had been using my throat as a coal-chute.

Under these conditions, we have kept the children back from the first and second days of term, which is probably a mistake, for they have recovered before us and their high spirits are beginning to have a deeply depressing effect on us. For a while, however, when the children were lethergic and sickly, I found the experience quite pleasurable, despite our discomfort. This may sound perverse, but I enjoyed the mutual dependency, the sense of being pulled together as a family, which illness forced on us. The children regress very quickly when they are sick, and indeed become like oversized babies, having to be carried and fed, and spending much of the time asleep. They are like babies too in that they do not look outside the family for amusement, or anything else. Though I recognize the unhealthy possibilities in relishing this situation, I can see no harm in making the most of it while it lasts: I have not felt as close to the children for many months, nor to Sally.

*

'Sally pregnant. Hurrah!' I wrote jubilantly in my diary for January 1977.

Within a day we had chosen the name Matilda, but with the strange provision that we would only use its diminutive, Tilly. This was Sally's choice and I was perfectly content with it, even after we discovered that it derived from an Old German name meaning 'strength in battle', which had an ominous ring to it. We toyed with a number of boys' names, but could not fix on one, and never took the search seriously. Sam, Dan, Jo, Nick and Tom all enjoyed brief periods of favour, but none endured. Why we fancied these plain, monosyllabic names, I do not know. I also entertained more florid ideas, for I was rather taken with Dickens's device of naming his children after his favourite writers. By and large his sons led unhappy and unsuccessful lives, and perhaps this was because they were not only crushed by a celebrated father, but burdened as well with such names as Alfred D'Orsay Tennyson, Edward Bulwer Lytton, Henry Fielding, Walter Landor and so on. Even Sydney Smith Dickens, whose name at least seems more propitious than the rest, was sent to sea where he acquired debts so enormous he was forbidden to return home. At any rate, I could not persuade Sally of the poetic ring to Oscar Wilde Harrison, Peter Kropotkin Harrison (I was going through an anarchist phase then) or Vladimir Nabokov Harrison. The names game never seems to lose its zest while pregnancy lasts, and we certainly played it continuously throughout the following months, but we never seriously reconsidered our first choice.

I am a believer in the Puritanical notion that there is, or ought to be, an equation between effort and reward, but this principle is utterly defied by pregnancy, for no act of creativity is easier to perform and none gives more gratification. Once Sally's test proved positive, and we never thought of it as more than an academic exercise, we were overwhelmed by our own sheer cleverness. We rejoiced in our extraordinary genius, we revelled in our sublime achievement. We rang and wrote to everyone we knew, trumpeting our brilliance, and received their congratulations in the spirit of Nobel Prize winners. Nothing happened to spoil our self-satisfaction: Sally was a little sick at first, felt a little pain and went through a brief period of lassitude, but she soon recovered, and thereafter spent the spring and summer ripening as perfectly and luxuriantly as a peach.

In our blithe way, we simply assumed that nothing would go wrong, that our baby would arrive on time (she did, to the day), that she would be perfect and that we would likewise make ideal parents. I have no idea where this lunatic confidence came from, unless it was somehow biologically induced and common to all prospective parents, but the fact was that, while neither of us could be accused of complacency in the ordinary way, during those nine months we were both ecstatically smug. We had the necessary money, we lived in the right house, and we were the right people to have a baby.

Or so we felt, though we were hardly justified, at least not in any rational sense, for the facts of our situation were open to a very different interpretation. My earnings were slender at best, and non-existent at worst. Our house was ramshackle, inconvenient, and lacking in every modern facility. We had no central heating and no washing machine, our water supply was far from reliable, and since we were on a month's notice we did not even have security of tenure. As to being the right people to become parents, I don't know what that means to this day, but if a proven record of stability in relationships had been a criterion, I would have failed to qualify. But then these things are not reducible to reason, and confidence in one's ability, however misplaced or unproven, is probably the best qualification of all. We only knew we wanted a child, and that she would be loved when she was born.

*

Instead of having a skull on my desk to act as a *memento mori*, I keep a drawing by Tilly, which bears the legend 'Do Not Smok'. Below is a hand with a cigarette between its fingers and an ashtray carrying a couple of squalid stubs. Inscribed in the ashtray is the grim warning 'You Will Die'. This was presented to me some time ago and it had its effect because although I did not stop smoking, I at least reduced it to one cigar a day.

Alas, my modest regimen could not withstand the strains of the last few months, during which I have been smoking cigarettes uncontrollably. To smoke, or not to smoke, has been the great dilemma of my life and I have never resolved it with any equanimity, even for a few months. When I smoke I feel guilt and disgust; when I don't, I feel starved and incomplete. Making tobacco both lethal and exquisitely pleasurable was surely one of the cruellest tricks played on suffering humanity by a malign fate. Why couldn't nature have behaved decently and given us a harmless narcotic?

Sally hates my smoking, and under her influence the children have learnt also to take a very puritanical line, which was graphically expressed in Tilly's bleak reproof. At Christmas this year I made a tremendous effort to return to my old cigar-a-day ration. Summoning the children to witness the start of my reform, I ceremoniously committed a half-full pack of cigarettes to the Aga, and together we watched it shrivel to ash in the coals. To ease myself into the new discipline, I bought a caber-sized Cuban cigar, which I smoked after Christmas lunch, devoting to the business of lighting it up all the pomp required by its immense size and price, and I succeeded in making it last throughout the afternoon and well into the evening. The children beamed in approval of this deliverance from sin, and they endorsed my good intentions by adding the cigar's aluminium tube and cedar-wood wrapping to their collection of treasures.

But, within three or four days, as I got back to work, the old desire for cigarettes began to prick and, inevitably, I succumbed. At first, I confined myself to smoking secretly in my room when the children were out of the house, My none-too-sensitive conscience being easily appeased with the delusion that this was, after all, a means of restricting my consumption. Soon enough, however, I grew careless and my crime was discovered. The children showed their anger by taking direct action. They simply threw my cigarettes in the bin. Being thoroughly readdicted by then, I was furious and frightened at the loss of my necessary fix.

My moral position is hopelessly riddled with hypocrisy. I cannot, will not, give up, but I loathe seeing the children playing with my cigarettes, pretending to puff them and generally imitating me. For, despite their disapproval of smoking in principle, they are nevertheless intrigued by its playful aspects. Jack is especially interested in my lighters and the paraphernalia of smoking, which to my cost I know is one of its seductive charms. Apart from wanting to protect them from the physical dangers of tobacco, I want to spare them the anguish of struggling to break a habit, which is viciously tenacious, but I suppose the most I can hope for is that my lamentable example will act as a deterrent.

I feel very bad about betraying my Christmas promise; I feel still worse about deceiving the children, who are so gullible. Though notoriously perceptive and observant in some ways, children are in other ways quite obtuse and blind. Even after they had realized I had begun openly to smoke once more, weeks went by without their noticing or objecting. In fact, it was only yesterday, a month after Christmas, that Tilly registered another serious protest. Seeing some cigarettes on my desk as she collected her things for school, she suddenly shouted at me not to smoke and put the packet in her satchel.

'I'm taking them away,' she said fiercely. 'You promised.'

'Please, don't. I will stop, but not today,' I said in a voice that was both wheedling and desperate.

'You'll die, you'll die,' she shouted. Usually her tone is schoolmarmish and she loves an excuse to play the adult with me, but on this occasion she was distressed, and truly meant what she said. She sank to the floor and began to cry. I did not know what to do, for I could not make an empty promise, yet I wanted to reassure her.

'I promise you I really am trying to smoke less.' This at least had some truth in it, which she seemed to believe.

She returned the packet and sat on my knee for a moment while I comforted her. Then she pranced off and left for school without a backward glance or any sign of unhappiness.

Strange to say, this concern for my health is, despite the 'Do Not Smok' notice, a new development. Indeed, there was a time when Tilly positively looked forward to my death.

'When are you going to die, Dad?' she would enquire brightly.

'Not for a long time, I hope.'

'Oh! Why not?'

This ghoulish exchange would take place quite frequently, and, naturally, it puzzled me, until I realized her interest in the imminence of my death was motivated by a curious belief she had formed that in order for her to take her place in the adult world I first had to vacate mine. She seemed to conceive of adulthood as a sort of bus with a limited number of seats. If I were selfishly to occupy my seat for too long, she would be forced to hang about in the queue of childhood, waiting impatiently for me to do the honourable thing. Why I should have been the obstacle to her growing up, and not Sally, I never discovered.

Jack did not share this belief in the finite space theory of adulthood, but, like her, he has no inkling of what death means, even though they have both known people who have died, in particular a little girl at their school who was tragically killed by cancer not long ago. All children seem to have a wonderfully blithe faith in their own immortality, which is no doubt as much a protective device provided by biology as the result of inexperience. If children were weighed down with a knowledge of the frailty of their existence – and their vulnerability to death is, after all, still greater than an adult's – they would never achieve their full potential as creative, imaginative beings, for they would be crushed with anxiety before they began. As it is, the phenomenon of death does not impinge on them as anything but a myth, a rumour, a misfortune that befalls other people but leaves them unscathed and unthreatened.

However, Tilly's new concern with my smoking is perhaps provoked by her fear of my making a different kind of departure, of my leaving again as I did in November, and it is this, rather than my death, that she is desperate to forestall. But I am only guessing; her thoughts concerning my desertion remain as unfathomable as ever, and I do not like to press her, for fear of raising anxieties that are now dormant.

The summer of Tilly's pregnancy was hot and friendly; Sally grew steadily rounder, finally achieving the beautiful globose shape of a water melon, and there was something profoundly satisfying in having our baby quicken in step with the farm crops surrounding our house. I, meanwhile, was undergoing a transformation of my own. The expectant father often shows a reaction to his wife's pregnancy, known as the couvade; it has not been much studied, perhaps because it manifests itself in curious and sometimes comical ways, which are not recognized for what they are. Deriving from the French word *couver*, meaning to hatch, it describes the father's impulse to identify with or imitate the pregnant mother. In some societies this impulse is acknowledged and catered for in ritualized form. I have seen film of fathers writhing and agonizing in mock labour while their wives underwent the real ordeal in the hut next door. To some degree the function of this ritual has been taken over in our society by fathers attending childbirth in hospital, but for the preceding nine months the couvade is left to its own devices, which may not be recognized for what they are.

I would guess that the most common expression of couvade in the middle-class father is to become knowledgeable, often to the point of being obnoxious, about every aspect of gynaecology and obstetrics, sickening dinner parties with his gruesome expertise in posterior presentations, cervical dilation, uterine contractions and so on. This was certainly the case with me, and I took pride in the fact that I knew far more about the mechanics of labour than Sally.

But there are other, less conscious forms of expression, in which a bizarre and uncharacteristic creativity emerges. For example, we knew a couple who lived quite happily in an undecorated house for years, but when the wife reached the eighth month of her pregnancy the husband suddenly began to paint the room destined to be the nursery. Unfortunately, the baby was born prematurely, and his decorating urge waned as quickly as it had sprung up, leaving the room half-painted and lumbered with open paint pots and dried-out brushes.

Just before Tilly was born, I embarked on a similarly doomed scheme. Overcome by an unprecedented burst of gardening enthusiasm, I built a rockery beneath a sycamore tree that stood sentinel at the far end of our lawn. With manic energy, I laid waste a jungle of weeds, hauled tons of rock, dug in bag after bag of peat and, at fabulous expense, planted out every variety of heather known to our local nursery. Then Tilly was born. The sycamore shed its leaves, burying the tender heathers in an acid shroud, and I forgot the whole project. By the following spring the heathers were all dead, and the rockery had come to resemble an inexplicable Neolithic monument, a mere riddle of scattered stones.

While waiting for Jack, I developed a longer lasting and altogether more rewarding mode of creativity. Under the tuition of a true maestro, I had already become interested in making wine, but in the last months of Jack's gestation, I began to produce the stuff on an industrial scale, filling row upon row of demi-johns with damson, plum, greengage, apple, pear, bullace, sloe and any other fruit I could lay my hands on. Soon enough the single-gallon demi-johns became too small for my purpose, and I expanded into five-gallon jars. Finally, I purchased a wonderful globular, grape-shaped glass carboy, whose capacity was a majestic ten gallons. This noble vessel was duly filled with plum wine and as Sally's belly swelled into a huge plum itself the cloudy liquor slowly cleared to attain a magically translucent purple. Here was my baby, my alternative production. Unlike Sally's baby, however, each stage of its maturation could be seen through the green skin of its glowing glass pod, and I did not hesitate to show it off.

Though the verdict of the amateur winemaker on his own products is notoriously untrustworthy, I nevertheless assert that Jack's vintage was delicious. Nor did I abandon my winery after he was born; indeed, I continued for some years, and only stopped when we moved here to this house.

All these activities can be made to seem absurd, but they mask something serious, something that is socially neglected, and, in most cases, personally ignored. Because the father's position in the family is still somewhat tangential, the prospect of becoming a father and the immediate event of pregnancy may well provoke a confused emotional response. Speaking for myself, I can say that my response was initially not at all confused, but grew to be so later. At first, I felt a tremendous surge of pride owing to the primitive affirmation of my virility and fertility. And I also felt proud of Sally on the same grounds. Though easily accomplished, our achievement was, after all, no small feat. To create life, to set in motion a new existence, is an awesome act to the individuals involved, no matter how commonplace or redundant it may be in the history of the species. Making a new life provides concrete confirmation of one's selfhood, one's manhood or woman-hood, of the need for one's own existence. On discovering that Sally was pregnant, I felt I knew who I was in a way that had not been so clearly defined by any previous experience.

But this euphoric stage did not last long; for then other, disturbing and ignoble sensations had to be digested. Just as getting married changes the quality of a relationship in some inexplicable but decisive way, no matter how long the couple have lived together, so it is subtly changed by the revelation of pregnancy. Obviously, it is in the woman that change most conspicuously registers itself: Sally's beloved body began to undergo a wonderful yet terrifying transformation, whose mystery was in fact not diminished one jot by my aggressive gynaecology. Pregnancy is a challenge to male authority, and the couvade is an expression of his resentment and jealousy; it is also an expression of male frustration in the face of a natural force he is helpless to control. It is an attempt to compete with a creativity he is quite powerless to rival, and a way of invoking magic to protect himself from a far stronger magic which has rendered him otherwise impotent. Apart from acting the provider, there is in reality next to nothing the man can do during pregnancy: he has no role but to watch and wait. However, this very lack of function, an experience which in itself is contrary to all the conventional patterns of manliness, provokes its own fear and bewilderment.

I am painting a rather monstrous portrait, which in most cases, including my own, is probably only the shadow side of much more positive and affectionate responses. Yet these phantom monstrosities are incubated alongside the real baby, and they are not always extinguished in the dawn of birth.

Tilly has just undertaken one of her perennial rearrangements of the furniture in her room; this time she has cleared the space to accommodate a dormitory for some of her dolls. Lined up with institutional precision along one wall are seven small beds, each immaculately made up and equipped with its own bedside box displaying an item of treasure. Installed in the beds are seven dolls, each lying prone and obedient, each primly attired for sleep. This regimentation and careful attention to detail are typical of her style of mothering, if that is the right word.

Ever since she has been able to play in any organized way, she has been preoccupied with dolls, and her interest first achieved its obsessional level in the latter months of Sally's pregnancy with Jack. She was deeply fascinated by the ever-swelling mound of Sally's stomach and whenever she had the chance she would stroke it, prod it, put her ear to it, and generally attend to its contents. Since the word 'baby' was constantly on our lips, it was not surprising that it was one of the first to enter her vocabulary. As with Jack later, the very first word she pronounced with any clarity was 'pig', and during that expectant January, when Jack's difficult gestation was reaching its end, pigs and babies dominated her imaginative world.

Her games were a mixture of imitation and compensation: she did to her dolls what was done to her, and in the process seemed to be restoring her own dignity. She fed them, gave them drinks, dressed and undressed them, changed their nappies, put cream on their plastic bottoms, carried them from one place to another and began the whole process again.

Watching her deal with her passive charges was salutary. Because of their size and frailty, small children and babies appear to be helpless in the hands of their parents, but the opposite is the case. To feed a one-year-old who has firmly clamped shut her mouth, who rolls her head from side to side as the spoon approaches, smearing food over her face and in her hair, who, despite being strapped into her chair, can still kick the bowl out of your hand, who will scream and cry during the strategic intervals when the spoon is not hovering, who will, if all else fails, choke and produce every sign of imminent death by asphyxiation – to feed such a beast calls for rare skill, patience and strength, as well as a willingness to engage in terrible violence. For small children have no fear of violent confrontation: ordinary civilities are thrown to the winds as they rage, shout, howl, lash out and fight to have their way. The adult emerges from these clashes of will bruised and distraught, having endured an emotional battering that only the worst marital row could inflict; the child, meanwhile, shakes off the incident and is immediately her usual sunny self.

What we saw in Tilly's games with her dolls was a silent parody of our methods, a kind of Chaplinesque version of parental care, in which everything was reduced to farcical, quick-time brutality. Assuming a complete lack of cooperation in her doll, she would hurl it to the floor, spreadeagle it, hold down its unresisting limbs with her knee, rip off its clothes and change its nappy as if restraining a lunatic in a strait-jacket. Throughout the operation, she would bellow, 'No, baby!' in its face, but in a matter-of-fact, almost jolly tone. It came as a relief to discover that she possessed this robust resilience to emotional strife, but at the same time it was shocking to realize how much of her life was passed in various states of petty humiliation. At sixteen months, she was still in nappies both day and night, and therefore subject to the interminable round of up-ending and stripping-off, which we were seeing reflected in her ferocious games.

In those days she had a small family of dolls, not at all on the scale of her present horde, and she had no particular favourites, preferring only to play with the smaller, more manageable ones. But throughout her entire life she has owned one doll, which is now her undoubted favourite, the crown princess of her household, and that is Emma, who was bought for Sally when she was a small girl.

For most of Tilly's life Emma has been her companion and *alter ego*, serving as friend, comforter, sister, child, serf and tool. At toy shops she is never forgotten; nor is she overlooked at Christmas when her card and presents are always thoughtfully chosen. She glides between fantasy and reality with an ease that can only be achieved by the truly archetypal, who lack all trace of personality. Tilly's games with her involve an indistinct blurring of the disingenuous and the magical. Emma is a prop to her identity, a bastion between her and the world, the chief victim of her power mania, the chief object of her overt affections, and her confidante and consoler. On occasions, she is also the instrument of knowing jokes played on baffled adults.

When we are late in the morning and breakfast is a maelstrom of spilt drinks, forgotten homework and lost satchels, Tilly will be discovered punctiliously installing Emma in her high chair and feeding her with exaggerated tenderness.

'Come on, Tilly. We're going to be late.'

'Emma's hungry,' she says, piously spooning another mouthful towards Emma's impassive lips.

'Tilly. Hurry up.' I speak through clenched teeth, and my tone is getting jagged with rage.

'Eat your lovely cereal,' coos Tilly gently, demonstrating through *her* tone the difference in our parental styles.

I crack.

'Put the damn doll away, and get on with your breakfast.'

'She's not a doll,' comes the inevitable retort. 'She's a little girl and she's very hungry.'

At this point I am defeated, because I know I will not rip through the fantasy, even though it is being used against me quite cynically. And so I grind my teeth in silent fury, and look on helplessly as Emma is treated to a full-scale breakfast.

Tilly's life-long attachment to dolls has been motivated as much by the desire to exercise power as by parental instinct, if the two are separable. Jack, by contrast, has never been interested in dolls as babies. He has always had a huge collection of soft toys and doll-figures, and he sometimes lavishes on them the same kind of domestic attention as Tilly does on her dolls, putting them to bed, arranging houses for them and so on. He also derives much infantile comfort from them and he too never sleeps alone. But, apart from his bears and other furry toys, which are treasured purely for their security value, the doll-figures he really likes, such as his A-Team manikins, all have some heroic quality to them. They are miniature, possessible versions of super-human beings, all masculine, with whom he identifies, and whose extraordinary powers he borrows in fantasy. They are relics of the true cross, fetish objects whose magic converts him into an irresistible, all-powerful god. In other words, he looks up to his toys, worshipping them as shadows of the charismatic superman he longs to become. For this reason he never objects to his soldiers, robot-monsters, knights, spacemen and so on being referred to as toys. They are just that to him, for the word *toy* does not diminish their magical associations.

Tilly, on the other hand, looks down on her dolls. The process is the same, but works the other way round: by being babies her dolls make her omnipotent, whereas if they were mere dolls, she would be no more than a little girl. His fantasies derive more from mythology than hers, but they are almost completely concerned with physical feats and the capacity for limitless destruction. He dreams of death rays, of driving cars that turn into rockets and travel at the speed of light, of costumes that give him Herculean strength, of felt-tip pens that are really sub-machine guns, of books that contain, as well as the funniest joke ever told, spells that will make him Master of the Universe. Though no less inspired by megalomania, Tilly's fantasies are concerned with imposing power through relationships, rather than muscular strength. Her caring and nurturing games, which hold no interest for him, are the means of manipulating her little court of babies, all female, according to her absolute whim.

As a baby herself, her attitude to other younger babies was always warm and very patronizing. She would pat them respectfully on the head, and ask to hold and rock them. At some level she must have felt threatened by her unborn sibling, and must have resented the incessant talk about babies that went on around her, but I think she also knew by then that babies were a good thing in that they made her look more grown-up. Her response to the threat was altogether healthy and creative: she produced a baby of her own. She would often come up to me holding out her doll and pointing to it. 'Baby, baby,' she would repeat again and again, until I acknowledged it and agreed that it was indeed a baby. This frequently enacted ritual seemed to confirm her own existence and importance, and she would signify her pleasure by closing both eyes, giving me a kind of slow-motion, double-barrelled wink.

Sally had enjoyed a summer pregnancy with Tilly; it had been an idyllic interlude and as painless as such an experience can be. Her pregnancy with Jack, however, was a winter affair, fraught with continual discomfort. His very inception had been clouded with anxiety and confusion. At first it was thought that Sally was not pregnant at all, for the embryonic Jack was identified as 'a growth'. This sinister diagnosis then gave way to the news that, although she was pregnant, the fertilized egg had failed to descend into her womb and was lodged in one of her fallopian tubes. While her pregnancy in fact marched on successfully, its progress was marked with a series of such gynaecological scares. Whether because of the worry induced by these crises, or because there really was some problem, which thankfully righted itself, Sally endured chronic distress throughout her nine months. Matters were made worse by the fact that our material situation was far less rosy than it had been during Tilly's pregnancy.

In that palmy summer we had been sustained by a plentiful supply of money and the delusions of happy ignorance. But by Jack's winter our money had run out, and we had encumbered ourselves with the first few links in the chain of debt which still shackles us to the bank. Delightful though Tilly was in every way, we now knew what having children involved, and it seemed as if our problems were about to be doubled. Sally continued to work at her restaurant in Bury St Edmunds, but with ever-increasing difficulty, and I had recently aborted a half-written book, without managing, as it were, to seduce my publisher into planting a new contract in my vacant womb.

Shortly before Christmas, the disaster we both dreaded appeared to strike. Sally lost a great quantity of fluid in the night. The doctor came, together with the local midwife, and to our horror an ambulance was summoned. Sally was made to sit in a canvas chair, wrapped in blankets, and was wheeled out of the house and up the ramp into the ambulance. A blanket was even put over her head, to protect her from the rain, but it made her look like a criminal. Tilly was unfortunately still awake and I held her in my arms as we stood in the porch, watching the blue light flash its eerie, circling glare round the pig yard. They closed the door on Sally, who was crying, and drove her away.

In the event, this proved to be yet another false alarm, and in a couple of days Sally was sent home to resume her ordeal of waiting. Tilly was for some reason more disturbed by her return than her departure. She cried for more than an hour, then fell asleep and did not wake until late the following morning. By way of a treat, she was taken to see Father Christmas in one of Bury's stores, and here she showed the recovery of her usual good humour by pulling his beard. Much to her amusement, this turned out to be attached to his ears by a length of elastic. She pulled it down to its full extent and let go, whereupon it flicked back and hit him in the eye. Despite his considerable pain and a rapidly closing eye, Father Christmas generously handed over the statutory gift.

We were warned that Jack, who was then to be named James, was likely to be premature by a month, a dangerous advancement, but although Sally's discomfort intensified, the baby settled and the crisis was postponed. I, meanwhile, had developed a sign of couvade sympathy, which while common was nonetheless unwelcome. Through this difficult winter I gradually added nearly two stone to my weight, the additional bulk gathering on my stomach as if I too were carrying a baby. Unlike a real mother, however, I did not shed my bulk when the baby was born but, if anything, continued to expand.

Towards the end of January, with only days to go before the predicted date of labour, Sally took to cleaning the house compulsively, being determined to have the place in a state of spotless readiness for the baby's arrival. Instead of a baby, snow came, rendering the farm and village very beautiful, but frightening us with visions of blocked roads and power failures. And so, day by day, the elephantine Sally groaned and panted as she scoured our already spotless house, while I, by then hardly less ponderous, brooded on our whitening landscape and waited. Tilly became increasingly obsessed with her dolls and added to Sally's burdens by teething. She also kept us awake at nights, for she returned to her infantile pattern of sleeping only in four-hour bursts, thus depriving Sally of the little sleep her pain and swollen belly permitted her. However, her pains did not turn into contractions and it seemed that the snow had frozen the baby into temporary inertia.

The saga of Jack's hole continues.

My theories concerning its psychological significance for Jack have not stood the test of experience, because it turns out that hole-digging exercises a universal fascination over boys. Jack's hole has become a local institution: since its initial excavation, we have been rung again and again with requests from his schoolfriends to 'come over Jack's', as they all put it, to play in his hole. It does not seem to hold the same attraction for girls, though Tilly herself has contributed quite as much as any boy to its creation.

Last weekend the children's cousins, Sal's sister's two boys, came to stay, and no sooner had they arrived than they were taken out to be shown the hole by torchlight. The following morning, Saturday, they woke at six-thirty, according to the boys' gruelling custom, but instead of disturbing us they dressed themselves and rushed out to the garden. When we finally got up, we went outside to find that it was a bitingly cold morning, but despite these conditions the children were still digging, and could not be persuaded to come in for breakfast. They were given sandwiches to eat on the site, but hardly touched them. By now the cavity had been doubled in width and depth, allowing all four to work inside with ease, and from my window I could only see the head of John, the eldest, on the rare moments when he paused in his labours to stand up. As the morning went on, the hole took on the grisly appearance of a mass grave dug out by its future occupants.

The temperature dropped, the puddles in our drive froze, and the occasional flurry of snow whipped across the bare face of the fields below, but the miners worked on, indifferent and oblivious. At one point Jack did return to the house, and I asked him if he was getting cold.

'No,' he said, 'I'm too hot,' and he ran upstairs to change into something cooler.

The analogy with a grave was reinforced. Halfway through the morning they stopped digging and began to put a roof over the pit, turning it into a sort of tumulus or barrow. They laid a couple of Sally's sheep hurdles over the top, dug a trench all round and heaped the earth over them in a great, swelling mound, leaving only a small, child-sized gap as entrance to the chamber. The chances of a burial were now all too real, for the roof was capable of caving in at any time and the hole had become a positive death-trap. But there was no deterring them: they worked with fiendish commitment, and it was well into the afternoon before they finally grew bored and turned to the alternative delights of throwing straw on my bonfire. By my calculations they had laboured without interruption for eight solid hours, thirty-two child-hours in all.

I still puzzle over the meaning attached to this hole-digging. For one thing, boys do not usually show these powers of long-term concentration on a constructive activity. As often as not, they will build something for a while, and then tear it down with the same gleeful energy. But Jack's hole has induced a quite different kind of interest, which so far has been continuously positive for more than a month. I cannot explain it, though I am convinced that a symbolic gesture is being made, which has ceased to be part of Jack's private world and has become a communal monument, celebrating some unintelligible boys' fantasy. His hole has acquired all the enigmatic grandeur of a Stonehenge.

*

Another month has gone by, putting that much more distance between us and the events of November. Sally and I are slowly drawing closer together and the children have almost dropped their campaign of reunification; however, a sad heritage of anxiety still haunts them.

This morning, as Sally was preparing to take them to school, Tilly made one of her few overt references to the situation. Misinterpreting the tone of Sally's parting words to me, which was in reality quite amicable, Tilly ran back into the house and dragged me out to the car.

'Give Mummy a special kiss,' she said urgently, 'she's got the hump.'

I did as I was told. In fact, I overdid it, because my attentions to Sally through the car window were greeted with a chorus of sniggers and wolf-whistles from the children in the back seat, though this was a sure sign of their approval.

For my part, I have begun to restore some of the old patterns of our life together, not out of guilt, or good intentions, but out of a genuine revival of love. I am once more reading to them every night; I am setting apart an hour or so of each evening to spend with them, if only watching television; I am joking with them again and hugging them freely. Sally has to go out tonight, and for the first time in many months, instead of dreading the prospect, I am looking forward to being with them on my own. These gestures may not seem to amount to much of an advance, but the fact is, as we are all discovering, the process whereby deep emotional hurts are healed is very gradual, and the slightest knock will reopen the wound. The children have one great advantage over us and that is that their anxieties come and go, and do not overshadow all their thinking. It is true that when they come, they do so with a terrible, smothering intensity, but when they go, they disappear completely for the time being, and lie, locked and dormant, in some cellar of their mind, leaving them carefree and confident. This, along with their inextinguishable optimism, is surely one of the most enviable blessings of childhood. Of course, the most potent source of consolation for the children is their growing belief in the stability, the mutual safety, of my relationship with Sally, and that is becoming more and more a reality, and less and less a front put on for their benefit. This winter does, after all, hold the promise of a spring.

FEBRUARY

By way of a portent rain fell on the night in 1977 when January turned into the February of Jack's birth; indeed, it rained so heavily that the curve of the road beyond our house, which forms a misplaced basin, became flooded, and we had to put out 'Slow' signs as a warning to drivers. When we woke the following morning almost all the thick snow had been washed away, leaving only a few liquifying patches to mark the heaviest drifts.

Sally's specialist told her that the baby was not due for a fortnight, but the foetal Jack had other plans. As if in sympathy with nature's deluge, Sally's waters broke in the early morning of the fourth. Tilly woke for her bottle at two o'clock, and forty minutes later Sally had her first contraction. Two more followed at ten-minute intervals and so we rang the hospital.

Owing to an industrial dispute, which had prompted a go-slow in the hospital laundry, patients were then being asked to bring their own towels, nappies, nightdresses and so on, but Sally was highly organized and had packed her emergency suitcase weeks before. Within minutes of speaking to the hospital, we were able to drive the still sleeping Tilly to a friend in the next village. She did not wake until we handed her over at the doorstep, and when she became aware of what was happening she seemed extremely pleased with her heroic role in our adventure, waving us off with royal condescension.

As on the previous occasion, it was a clear, moonlit night, though our mood was very different. This time our minds were anxiously locked in the present, for we were worried about Tilly and her reaction to a new sibling, about all the other arrangements we had made to keep the house going in our absence, and, above all, about Sally's forthcoming ordeal, concerning which we knew too much to revive our first naive excitement.

By the time we reached the hospital, Sally's contractions were coming every two minutes, and the porter pushed her in a wheelchair to the delivery suite. I saw her into her room and was then despatched, somewhat officiously, to the cheerless waiting room. It was four-forty when I saw her again. She had been given Pethidine and had been told that her labour was already in its last stages. She did not fall asleep between contractions or become delirious, but remained lucidly con-versational throughout. I sponged her head and held her hand.

Despite its bad moments, Tilly's birth had been a pro-foundly rewarding experience, on which we both looked back in our different ways with wonderment and pride. Jack's birth, however, was, like his pregnancy, overshadowed by too many fears to be moving. At every stage we were only conscious of being relieved that none of the predicted dangers had in fact come to pass. Our sense of apprehension was not eased by one member of the staff, the woman who had rushed me into the waiting room. Her professional skill could not be faulted, but her attitude to Sally and labouring mothers in general was highly unsympathetic. Throughout she addressed Sally as 'pet', 'petal', 'your missus' and so on, but never by her name. The same patronizing, almost contemptuous approach led her to treat Sally with a cold efficiency that was never mitigated by any explanations or reassurance. At one point she rebuked Sally for crying out, telling her that she must remain quiet for the sake of the girl next door who was having her first baby and would be frightened by the screams of other mothers.

'You should know better,' she said. 'This isn't your first.'

'I'm not going to have any more,' was Sally's pathetic response, as she struggled with a painful contraction.

'Very well! We'll get doctor to sew you right up, shall we?'

Later she had to leave our room to take a phone call from a mother whose labour was just beginning. When she came back, she announced, 'One of these days we'll just tell them we're closed and that will be that.'

All these sardonic remarks were intended as jokes, but it seemed to us they masked a dreadful impatience. No doubt we were being oversensitive, but I am sure she had been too long in the job and had lost that necessary identification with the patients in her care. At all events, her brisk indifference to Sally's state of mind made an unhappy contrast with the kindness and understanding shown by the staff who had attended Tilly's birth at the same hospital.

After some minor difficulties, which threatened to be much worse than they were, Jack was expelled at great speed at 6.43, according to one of the few notes I managed to make. Poor Sally suffered far more pain than she had with Tilly, but her labour was, mercifully, four hours shorter. The aftermath of his birth was also far less painful and problematic. Within an hour she had been stitched and was sitting up, in relative comfort, giving Jack his first feed. Within a mere thirty-six hours she was released from hospital and back home.

Jack's birthday fell on a Tuesday this year, so we arranged to have his party on the previous Sunday morning.

The weather proved to be cruelly cold, but the dozen or so boys who assembled with their bikes were not deterred. With the exception of only one tearful victim of the Arctic chill, in whom I recognized my own childhood self, the guests entered heartily into the spirit of this unusual party, which at Jack's request consisted of bike scrambles through the wood and races up and down our drive.

At one stage they were required by Sally, the games leader, to make timed runs across the garden and round the back of the barn. We were puzzled at first by the length of time it took these demon racers to complete the final leg of the route, from which they all emerged with reddened faces and extra coats of mud. However, we then discovered that Tilly and her permitted quota of two girls were hiding behind the barn where, out of our sight, they were pushing the boys off their bikes as they rode by. The boys were furious, but too proud to admit to the ignominy of their downfall.

Later, they broke for a while to play an impromptu game of football. I came out of the house to see Jack dribbling the ball across the lawn. He retained possession with rare skill, but kept shouting in an anguished voice, 'Where's the goal, where's the goal?'

At about half past eleven they sat down to a traditional birthday tea of crisps, orange squash and cake, which Sally had made in the shape of a ghost, eerily iced in white with an electric blue sash. Jack seemed mightily pleased with the whole event, which was indeed a triumphant affair.

For his actual birthday, he insisted the night before that we set his alarm to ring at the exact moment of his becoming seven years old – 6.43 a.m. In the event he was awake and alert well before six, and we had to make him lie in our bed while we vainly attempted to go back to sleep. Every five minutes he plaintively demanded to know the time, but we waited for Tilly's digital alarm to wake her and announce the precise anniversary of his birth.

I was dreading the opening of his parcels; we were undergoing one of our perennial cash crises and had been forced to buy him only a few small, cheap toys, but in his good-natured way he thanked us again and again for what he was given. If he was disappointed, he showed no sign of it.

After bringing Sally and the new-born Jack home from hospital, I drove to collect Tilly in time to see her new brother. We had laid our plans in order to give her the best possible introduction to this potential usurper of the throne on which she had reigned with such carefree majesty all her short life. We were both very nervous about her response to Jack, fearing that she might feel supplanted, and fearing too that our affection, which had been lavished exclusively on her for seventeen months, might not stretch to Jack, or might be transferred entirely to him, or might be divided unevenly. My own particular fear was that Jack would never achieve the same importance in my feelings as Tilly, whom I had come to love with a ferocious intensity. I had always listened with horror when other people talked of having their 'favourites', but now Jack was born I suddenly discovered the same capacity in myself and I was determined that it should not be realized.

Alas, our plans were scuppered by Tilly herself, who fell asleep in the car as I brought her back. I carried her upstairs to her bed, and found that Jack was also asleep in his basket. The house was serenely peaceful, and Sally was delighted to be walking around her own kitchen once more, feeling next to no discomfort despite her eight stitches.

This idyll was not prolonged. Tilly woke an hour later and insisted on making her inspection of Jack, though she looked very tired and was red in the face, always an ominous sign. I brought her downstairs and Sally lifted her up to look at the still sleeping Jack. She said 'baby' in a very solemn tone, and patted his head. Sally pointed out his eyes and ears, and she touched them gently and repeated the words. She stroked his hair repeatedly, saying 'Jack' after us. She put her doll, a new one, beside him in his basket.

She was, inevitably, a little clumsy and we struggled to restrain her rougher gestures, without giving her the feeling that we valued him too highly for her to touch. Our feelings were very mixed: we desperately wanted this moment to go well for her, but we did not want her to wake him, for a sleeping baby gives such precious relief to exhausted parents. We were also still in that very early phase of thinking that the slightest knock would break a limb or snap his head off his little pipe-stem of a neck.

This crucial first meeting appeared to be successful, until fatigue suddenly overwhelmed her. She began to cry and tried to climb into his basket. When we took her away, she cried all the more violently and became very upset. Sally carried her back upstairs, but could not persuade her to get into bed. She held on to Sally tightly and dragged her down to lie on the carpet. Finally, still sobbing, she did fall asleep, her head nestled on Sally's now deflated stomach. Just as Sally was about to lift her into bed, she woke for a moment and prodded her stomach to make sure the bulge had not returned.

The next morning she was the last to wake, and Sally was feeding Jack by the time she tottered through to our room. When I came back upstairs with the tea I found all three in bed, Tilly looking very pleased, as if the baby were hers, and holding a possessive arm round his lolling head. Once he was asleep, we put him back in his basket, which did not please her, because she could not see easily over the edge, and once more she tried to clamber in beside him. We let her help to put the blankets round him, a task she performed with assiduous care, though for some unfathomable reason she protested tearfully to an eiderdown being put over him and flung it aside.

Later, when she saw Sally making up a bottle of sugared water for him, she grabbed it for herself and drank the lot, but this was the only real gesture of jealousy she made while he was a baby. From then onwards, apart from occasionally landing a sly blow on his head when she hoped we weren't looking, she showed him nothing but the most absorbed and affectionate interest, and quickly formed a sort of collusive infant solidarity with him. She developed only one unfortunate way of paying him attention, which I have seen in other small children dealing with babies, and that was to poke her fingers in his eyes. I am sure this was not done out of any desire to hurt him, rather, it was an attempt to get in touch, literally, with the only truly expressive part of his face. Of course, babies express themselves all too effectively with their mouths when they bawl, but otherwise, until they learn to smile, their expressiveness is mostly confined to their eyes, which, when they do focus and are not rolling around their heads like fish in a bowl, stare at the world with a look of stunned wonderment.

Jack was a pound and half heavier at birth than Tilly had been, but we had forgotten the minuteness and seeming fragility of new babies. His miniature proportions made Tilly, who was and probably always will be a miniature herself, seem momentarily Amazonian. Like her at that age, he tended to frown in horrified disbelief when his gaze locked on to our faces. His frowns were made doubly formidable by his hair, which from the start grew thickly on his cuboid head in a spontaneous crew-cut, giving him the look of a particularly hawkish American general. For the rest, he communicated by means of sneezes, cavernous yawns which seemed to open up his whole head, and strange little mewing cries. In those very early days, he was a grave, almost melancholy baby. As our first child, Tilly had more or less created her world, but his was ready-made, its lineaments laid down, its ritual already well worn, and this perhaps explains his solemn outlook, which is still natural to him.

I am looking out on a snowbound landscape, which gives me no pleasure at all. I cannot see its beauty for thinking of the ruinous expense we will incur to combat the cold and the ceaseless trouble we will have with our senile car, which suffers from a mechanical version of hypothermia and is unlikely to survive another hard winter. To the children, however, snow represents a gift from nature, uniquely designed for their amusement. Jack has a friend staying this week, and the three of them spend every available minute before breakfast and after school out on the tundra that surrounds our house. Snow, like sand, water and mud, offers them an irresistible and inexhaustible medium for play: they slide on it, roll in it, build with it, throw it at each other, eat it, or simply run about on it, screaming and rejoicing.

Not content with sand-bagging every room downstairs with heaps of sodden, icy clothes whenever they come in, they also leave all the doors open, which would be a crime in any house, but in a house without central heating is a capital offence. Worse still, when they rushed in this morning to make their breakfast – dawn had hardly broken and we were still cringing in bed – they burnt their toast and felt it necessary to open all the windows to let out the smoke. They were outraged when I told them off.

'We were only trying to help,' Tilly said, genuinely astounded at my temper.

Whether it is psychological or physical, I cannot tell, but children enjoy an impermeable protection from the cold, which evolution has denied the adult system.

Ten days after Jack was born, the snow, which had thawed

for our convenience, fell again, but this time in Alpine quantities, lying a foot deep in the garden and ten feet or more where drifts formed. Bury St Edmunds was reported to be cut off, and we had no post or milk deliveries. It was around this time that I finally realized where the centre of our universe lay: it was not in London, nor even Bury, but in Stowlangtoft itself. Remoteness is, after all, an entirely reversible concept. Who is remote from whom? When we first left London for the outer darkness of East Anglia, people, that is Londoners, used to ask how it felt to be so far away. Although the question always annoyed me, I accepted its premise and would protest that Suffolk was hardly Siberia, that we were only two hours from Liverpool Street Station, and so forth. But then, as our roots here began to deepen and spread, as I discovered that rural facilities were in many ways more efficient than metropolitan ones and were certainly pleasanter to use, and as London's allegedly civilized charms began to look more and more barbaric, I came to think that it was the capital, not the country, that was in exile. Of course Sally, in her wisdom, had always known this simple truth, but it was not until that winter's snow finally isolated London from Stowlangtoft that I knew I was a fully fledged parochial chauvinist.

The weather took us by surprise and on the first day of the big fall I heroically walked to Norton, a trek of some six miles there and back, to collect supplies. Overnight the village had been transported to Lapland: instead of the usual juggernauts, the street was full of people wrapped in furs and balaclavas, hauling their groceries home on sledges, their children perched on top of the boxes. The following day the milk van got through to our village shop and each household was allowed to pick up its allotted quota of bottles. Our quota was six, but I slipped and fell on the way home, and only managed to return with three pints. The cold was so extreme that Tilly and I were forced to give up our customary visits to the pig house.

However, the sows out in the paddocks were not deterred; they ambled all day in the snow, their mountainous dignity quite unaffected, though to our anthropomorphic eye their pink skins looked wretchedly naked. By now Sally was being hurt by her stitches, which were due to be taken out by the local midwife, but she could not get through, and poor Sally had to resign herself to suffering for the duration.

She was having to endure another kind of pain as well, because nursing Jack was making her very sore, and every feed was becoming an ordeal. Her pain communicated itself to Jack, who would not suck properly and was never fully satisfied. He chomped desperately on his dummy, but when presented with the real thing he would turn away and shriek. With Tilly, she had hardened her nipples with whisky, but this primitive anaesthetic brought no relief to her now, and its taste seemed to repel him still more. And so, he would cry.

A baby's crying is a unique form of expression, for it is both the product of suffering and the means of inflicting it on others, and when a baby cries persistently and inconsolably there is no parallel in human relations with the two-way torture that must be endured. His distress cannot be ignored, but nor can it be alleviated. His demand for help and attention electrifies the mother with a terrible charge of anxiety, but her efforts to relieve him and herself are doomed. His crying intensifies, his back arches, his legs stiffen, his arms thrash and his face turns purple; his entire being and body seem to contract to a howling hole of misery. She picks him up, rocks him, pats his back, strokes his head; she puts him down and tries to make him comfortable; she walks him round, attempts to feed him again, changes his nappy, lies down with him on the bed; she leaves him alone and shuts the door on him; she rescues him and straps him to her while she makes a cup of tea for herself; she coos at him, smiles at him, screams back at him, and shakes him, and cries herself. But nothing she does stops his relentless, inescapable crying.

By now the baby has turned into a complete stranger. All babies are strangers to some degree: they are unknown, and cannot be known, for their characters are not formed and as yet consist only in the most elemental impulses – desire and pleasure, fear and frustration, rage and pain. They are humanity reduced to its bare fundamentals, and there is a baby still howling and smiling inside all of us. But a crying baby is also inhuman: it becomes a mechanical source of noise that is both intolerable and unappealable, like a low-flying jet or a road drill. He is beyond the power of language and gesture; he will not respond to the great consolers of food, drink, sleep and warmth; he is a beast that will not be tamed. And it soon becomes difficult not to read obstinacy and malevolence in his crying: he is doing it deliberately, with an understanding of the stress he is causing.

His mother suffers from the most acute claustrophobia, all her powers of attack and defence are rendered futile. She is the victim and the cause of his pain, and her sense of inadequacy becomes as unbearable as her sense of being assaulted. Such unmitigable anguish is hardly ever experienced in ordinary life, and without turning to grotesque extremes it is impossible to find analogies. A torturer deals with lingering pain, but then he induces it and has the power to stop it. Firemen and doctors rescuing people from accidents confront agony, but they have effective means of relief, and though they may feel guilty about failing to alleviate suffering, they do not feel responsible for having caused it. Mothers feel guilty on both counts.

What mark does this chronic anguish leave on the baby himself? Nothing stands between him and his pain; it is simply felt, without any consoling knowledge that it cannot last forever, that someone or something will intervene in the end, that all things are relative. He cannot seek relief by diverting his mind elsewhere or occupying himself; he has no optimism or pessimism, no bright future to look forward to, no comforting past to look back on. He simply is his pain. I suppose it is impossible to uncover our earliest sensations and evaluate their effects. A kindly amnesia keeps them shrouded in the fog of prehistory before the dawn of memory. Yet surely our irrational dreads and fears have their origin in these bouts of infantile pain, whose sense of absolute suffering we never want to feel again.

And what mark does it leave on his mother (or father for that matter)? Her best efforts have failed to bring any comfort, and have instead only provoked aggression on a scale that the most brutal husband would think twice about inflicting. The baby converts his bad feelings into a terrible weapon of violence, which his mother is powerless to combat and has probably never faced before in her life. Overwhelmed by the sheer physical force of his crying, and horrified by her own uselessness as a mother, which seems to be putting the very existence of her child at risk, she soon reaches the limit of her resources. From this desperation, it is only a short step to taking up violence herself, if only to bring a moment's silence into the house and win a little respite. Some mothers do hit their babies; some shut them away to 'cry themselves out'; and most just struggle on until the baby does at last fall silent. But whatever the resolution, it must always be at severe cost to their self-esteem and self-confidence.

Yesterday my attention was caught by a sudden movement at the neck of our drive where it leads on to the little apron of parking space in front of my window. A young rabbit, no more than three weeks old, had run out of the wood to my right and was careering back and forth across the drive. Pursuing it was a small, brown creature, so low-slung I did not see it at first, but which proved to be a stoat, recognizable by its bounding movements and snow-white chest. It chased the rabbit down to the side of the hedge leading to our house and then hesitated as the rabbit came close to our front door. The rabbit ran out of my view, and the stoat, too frightened to go any closer to human habitation, stopped and slunk back into the wood. The rabbit seemed to have escaped, but then it too must have lost its nerve, for it reappeared and stupidly followed the stoat into the brambles. A minute later, the chase began again. This time right beneath my window, the stoat caught up with its victim, grabbed its back leg, tripped it and struck at the rabbit's furry throat. There was a terrible squealing, and the two bodies bowled over and over in the mud, the stoat digging its teeth deeper into the rabbit with each tumble. The rabbit stopped fighting, but lay twitching and writhing, and then at last fell still. With furious little jerks, the stoat began the laborious business of dragging the rabbit's heavy body back to its lair in the undergrowth, where perhaps its mate was suckling her young.

The rabbit's fate appeared to be sealed, but ten minutes later, to my surprise, it reappeared in the drive. It lay quivering on the ground, sprang up to take three or four steps, and flopped over as if tripped. The stoat had obviously injured its motor system in some way, but had failed to sever the big vein in its neck. Nor had the rabbit been 'stoated', that is terrified to the point where it becomes paralysed and simply waits for death, motionless and screaming. This young rabbit had not succumbed to fear and was doing its crippled best to escape. I could not understand why the stoat did not come out to recapture what was now the easiest prey, for they are known to be relentless hunters, never missing their kill once they have marked out their victim.

The rabbit was surely doomed. Even if the stoat had for some reason been deterred, some other predator, a fox, an owl or even a weasel, would make a quick kill of prey in that vulnerable condition. When next I looked up I could see no sign of the rabbit or its would-be executioner. I walked out and searched the brambles, but still could find no trace of them.

Later, when they came back from school, I described this incident to the children. Their reaction was a mixture of horror and fascination.

'Was there any blood?' Jack asked. I told him I hadn't seen any.

'Poor little bunny,' was Tilly's comment, but not said in a sugary way.

'Do you think he really died?' she asked me, and I told her I didn't see how it could have survived.

''Orrible old stoat,' was their final verdict, though they wanted to know if you could keep a stoat as a pet. They also wanted to be shown the exact spot where the rabbit had been attacked, which they studied closely for traces of gore, and they dragged me to see a small hole where the desiccated corpse of an adult rabbit lay. This, according to them, was a grave dug by another rabbit in which to bury its dead friend. The idea of death without burial is as shocking to them as it is to me, an incompleteness that should always be rectified.

Sally, in her own eccentric way, is the most enterprising woman I know. At the moment she is dividing her time between working as a casual decorator in a pub, which is under renovation, working with a thatcher as his 'toad', the craft jargon for assistant, and looking after her small flock of nine ewes and a ram, which she has just moved into a yard next to our house in preparation for lambing.

She has always worked and has pursued a bewildering variety of careers. There is, for instance, now no part of a pub in which she has not worked, from its kitchen to its bar, its roof to its cellar. And she must be one of the few caterers who can turn from preparing canapés to delivering a breeched lamb. When the children were very young she was running the bar and restaurant in the Theatre Royal, Bury St Edmunds's delightful Regency theatre. Prompted partly by our need of money, and partly by her reluctance to abandon a thriving business, she was determined to return to work as soon as possible after Jack's birth. And so, on only the sixteenth day of his life, she drove off after tea to rejoin her partner at the restaurant, leaving me in sole charge of the children for the first time.

Everything went smoothly, and I shall never forget the swelling sense of pride I felt as I sat in my study that night, rejoicing that I, and I alone, had successfully fed and got to sleep our two babies. This may seem a small thing, but anyone who has done it single-handedly will know that there are few achievements which are as testing to perform, or as satisfying to bring off. However, I was soon to be undone by overconfidence. On the third night I ignored the golden rule of planning well ahead, and hysteria broke loose. Having put a contented Tilly to bed, I came downstairs to find that Jack was awake and soaking wet all the way up his back. I left him in his basket and went upstairs to find him a dry set of clothes, but could find nothing suitable. I could not see into the cupboard properly, but dared not turn on the light for fear of waking Tilly. Downstairs, Jack was crying. I grabbed a handful of clothes and ran down to him. I began to change him, but realized I still had no vest so I carried him half-naked back upstairs where I crammed him into his new outfit. Working in the half-dark and shouting at him not to wake Tilly, I failed to ram his rubbery little arm into the sleeve of his babygrow. I was frightened of breaking it, but desperate to save him from getting any colder, and in my haste I must have hurt him, for he suddenly began to howl in earnest. Tilly woke, as she was bound to do, and struggled out of her bed to grab his hand and shout "Ello, 'ello' in his ear, while rubbing the top of his head, which was her method of soothing him. I bundled him down-stairs once more, knowing that meanwhile there was not a chance of Tilly staying in her bed, and put on the kettle to warm his milk. Tilly joined us and as I attended to her I allowed the bottle to get too hot. He was hungry and sucked furiously when I gave it to him, but burnt his mouth. I cooled the bottle and tried to persuade him to take it again, without success. He held his arms over his mouth and I had to force the bottle through. After a brief fight, he accepted it, but sucked so hard he choked. Tilly, in an attempt to assist, jammed it back in his mouth, which not only made him choke worse, but bruised his burnt lip.

At that moment, to my indescribable relief, Sally returned. She fed him, re-dressed him, installed him in his seat, put Tilly to bed and generally restored us to order.

When in a state of equilibrium, Jack's natural expression was one of profound anxiety, which only faded when he fell asleep. Awake, he would stare indifferently at us, the television and the wallpaper without giving any sign of recognition or response, except to furrow his brows and wring his hands compulsively. I used to stare back at him, wondering what was the source of this terrible uneasiness: he was fed, warm and comfortable, but his physical contentment only seemed to free his mind for still sharper, abstract worries. As with Tilly when she was that age, I was always glad to see his head droop and his eyes close; then we were both relieved of our anxieties for a while. Yet even when he was asleep, I used to think of him as a hand-grenade with the pin out, for it was only a matter of time before he exploded.

I think – and earnestly hope it is so – that the children have finally forgiven me for leaving in November. I said earlier that children tend not to bear grudges or nurse resentment, and I am still sure that it is true. On the other hand, they do have a powerful instinct for self-protection, which leads them unconsciously to withhold a part of their affection when they fear it is not going to be returned in equal measure. My children have never punished me for my desertion, though Jack has often made his disapproval clear, and I would never have noticed this reservation of their love if they had not suddenly, during the last week, shown me a small, but unmistakable increase in affection. I don't know whether they have discussed me and this is the production of some joint decision; I suspect not. In certain respect they are like twins, for they act and feel in concert without having to say a word, or exchange a glance. Sometimes their mutual spontaneity is really the result of imitation, working to and fro between them; sometimes, however, it seems to be the result of a more mysterious symbiosis, whereby the emotions felt by one are immediately communicated to the other and felt with the same intensity.

At all events, whatever its source or inspiration, this new edge of affection had been given to me by both, together and separately. Only yesterday Tilly caught hold of me and, quite unprompted, kissed me passionately, telling me I was 'a lovely Daddy', which was very sweet music. Jack has throughout been more overt with all his feelings, and has not ceased to offer me affection, both verbal and physical, but during the last week he too has added an extra degree to the warmth of his fondness. I have no doubt that some of the initiative has come from me as well. Although unaware of doing it, I must be indicating that I have become more receptive to their gestures. But, for all that, the new tone is of their making and I can only be grateful.

In many ways their relationship is like a marriage: they share so much, they are so often and for so long in each other's company, and they are required to accommodate so flexibly to each other's demands and whims, while yet maintaining their own identities and pursuing their own interests. There are of course plenty of differences, not least the fact that they do not have to deal with the complications of sex, yet the analogy still holds good, and we always marvel at the subtle and sinuous ways their lives intertwine. They do argue and fight and irritate each other, and no sound grates on my ear more than Tilly's wail of protest, when she manages to turn 'Jaaa-aa-aak' into a three-syllable word, but these clashes are always short-lived, if fiery, and never develop beyond bickering into serious antagonism. For the rest, their relationship is a model of harmony and good humour.

They have been ill recently, coming down in turn with a disgusting virus that made them vomit repeatedly and then fall into a prolonged sleep, from which they woke purged and refreshed. Fortunately, they are old enough to have the self-control to be sick in the loo, but they were a sorry sight during this phase, their faces turning the colour of ivory just before each attack. Both were very concerned when the other was in the throes of the plague. Jack's style of caring was to pursue her with a large plastic bowl whenever she moved, and to mummify her in blankets whenever she lay down, for he had heard that the victim had to be kept warm. Tilly's approach was more spiritual than practical: she stroked his head and gazed solicitously at him, but did not actually do much. In both cases, however, there was no mistaking the real anxiety they felt for each other.

He has never known a world without her, and she is almost as much a part of his existence as his own arm or leg. I doubt if she has any memory of the sixteen months when she was undisputed queen, though as an elder child she possesses a certain strength of character, not to say ruthlessness, which he lacks. And he, as a second child, has a moderation and willingness to bend which she lacks; he is also more clownish. They are, in other words, a good match, and in many ways their marriage runs in parallel with ours, for as often as not Sally and I confront them as one couple dealing with another. The warmth between them and their sense of solidarity has stood them in good stead over the last few months; although their anxieties seem to be more the product of solitary worrying, they have nevertheless clung together, giving each other a kind of mutual support we could never provide.

(These events, incidentally, must have taken a stiffer toll on me than I realized, because someone asked me today what I did with my time now I was retired!)

MARCH

We are still in the grip of winter, but signs of an imminent spring are everywhere, both outside and inside the house.

The punishing cold of the last few weeks has finally relented; it no longer stings to get out of bed, and the insides of our bedroom windows are not obscured by ice each morning. The first snowdrops are showing themselves around the bole of our horse chestnut tree, though as yet their petals have not sprung from the spear-heads of their sepals. The trees along our drive are tinkling with the songs of birds, mostly chaffinches, which flocked together in little fluttering clouds when the ground was hard and food scarce.

As soon as the earth lost its macadam of frost, a tractor appeared, lumbering across the field in front of our house like some prehistoric beast newly woken from hibernation and hungry for its first spring meal. In less than a morning it ploughed in the rotting sugar beet tops and turned our immediate landscape into a brown plush of turned soil. The pheasants and even a few wild duck had been feeding there during the harsh weather, but now they have fled the soft, clogging earth, leaving it to the seagulls, which wheel and dip in search of worms. However, for us the most conspicuous sign of the coming spring is the presence of Sally's ewes and ram behind our barn. The ewes are due to lamb late this year, on the sixteenth of this month, and they are looking rotund and sluggish, while their behaviour is unusually docile. Every morning and afternoon, Sally leads them out of their pen on a short jog round the house for the good of their health, but they have no enthusiasm for exercise and will go no further than the first patch of lawn, which they crop with furious greed. They take no notice of the children's waving and screaming, and only respond to the rattle of Sally's bucket as she pours out their concentrate food. Blowing heavily, they sprint back into their yard and jostle to get their heads into the trough.

Inside, there is a feeling of renewal too. In more senses than one, this has been the hardest winter of the children's lives, and we are looking forward to the spring with much more than ordinary, seasonal hope. Sally and I continue to puzzle over what I did in November, but to tell the truth, despite the many, many hours of talk we have had, I still do not really understand my actions or their causes. Obviously, there were factors in our relationship and in both our characters that made for difficulties in our marriage, and these we have endlessly discussed, but none of them, together or separately, now seems to amount to a reason for leaving home.

But then the conscious, rational mind, in my case at any rate, turns out to be a thin and fragile crust capping the molten turmoil of the unconscious, which occasionally erupts with shattering effects. For the most part, this volcanic pressure is harmlessly eased and tapped through the steady expression of words – writing. However, I do not understand and do not care to brood too intensely on the process whereby my work is produced. It is true that the structure of my life is now arranged around the presumption of writing – contracts, deadlines, promises of money to bank managers, a study full of books, a smoothly humming electric typewriter, a reputation to maintain, ambitions to fulfil, ideas to realize and so on – but none of these brings into existence a single word. That process remains mysterious, more like a physical than a psychological function. Words, ideas, images rise to the surface like gas-laden bubbles from the intestines of a bog. Once they have broken the surface and emerged into the clear atmosphere of consciousness, the raw gas is purified and refined through writing, and then, suitably bottled, is distributed to other people as fuel to warm their minds and imaginations. But while I understand how to treat and manage this gas in the laboratory of my rational mind, how to convert the crude, volatile fumes into a stable liquid under the pressure of art, I have no understanding of the inscrutable gastric workings of the unconscious that cause the creative belch to eruct in the first place.

Just as my professional life is based on the assumption of creative vitality, so our family life, which is far more ramified, with its possessions, routines, responsibilities and living fruits, is predicated on a belief in the endurance of love. And yet this structure that looks and feels so indestructibly solid when animated by love, turns out to be frail and illusory when love fails or is withdrawn. But is love subject to the same unfathomable spontaneity, the same organic quickening energy? Surely not.

Perhaps most other people are better able to control their internal turbulence; perhaps the lid of their conscious selves is thicker and fits more securely than mine; perhaps they show more restraint, more maturity, more moral self-discipline than I do. All I know is that in November I was overpowered by a terrible urge to desert and destroy, which I could no more understand than resist. And once I had left, I felt myself driven back by an equally irresistible urge.

Although I would hardly prescribe such a course to anyone else, and will never repeat it myself, some good has come out of it, for Sally and I are closer than ever before, and my love for the children radiates with all its old warmth. Now, the only real anxiety comes from not being able to explain my actions and their motives. The force of those conflicting urges that drove me from the house, and just as surely drove me back, did not connect with any of the problematic features of our married life; it seems to have been generated by some deeper, darker source. When emotions are creative and loving, one does not seek explanations, though their source is mysterious too, and defies rational probing; but when they are perverse and malign, they are made all the more dangerous for being unintelligible. I was never in any doubt as to where my duty lay, and I knew I was flouting it, but on returning I also knew that I would not for long be able to fulfil my duty emptily; to be meaningful, it had to be fused with feeling. But would duty alone inspire feeling? If I respected the outward form of marriage and family, for duty's sake, would love return to fill it from within? I cannot answer these questions, except to say that in my case, once the crisis had passed and I was back home, love began to gush from me as if it had been blocked and was now flowing under unusual pressure. Love and duty certainly coincided, but the springs of feeling and their ways of working remained as mystifying as ever.

Fortunately, children do not look for explanations; all they crave is the even perpetuation of the norm, and they were very happy to see us return to it, without wanting to question the disruption. They have never asked me why I went, and have only sought reassurance that I won't go again. Now that Sally and I are no longer giving out signs of anything but a unified relationship, they are beginning to put the whole disturbing episode from their minds. Its inexplicable aspects hold neither interest nor anxiety for them; they simply want to forget.

Last night we came home quite late, for the children, from having drinks with Sally's parents, and Sally immediately took Tilly upstairs to get her into bed. Jack, however, insisted on my taking him to inspect the sheep, for this was the predicted day of the first possible lambing. He also wanted an opportunity of testing the new torch his grandpa had just given him. To his astonishment and great delight, his torch beam did indeed reveal a lamb, a grey, bloodstained bundle trembling on the floor of what is usually our garage. One look was enough to send him running back to the house, shouting for Sally.

He made a touchingly comic sight: on his sizeable head, which when running he holds thrust forward as if in readiness to smash through road-blocks, he wore an old deer-stalker hat, pulled well down so that his ears projected at right angles. Incongruously combined with this gentlemanly headgear was one of his many militaristic jackets, which made him an honorary member of the SAS or some other bloodthirsty unit. And on his feet, as befitted a great warrior, he wore his slippers.

At his summons, Sally rushed from the house, pursued by Tilly, now in her nightdress. Back in the garage, we discovered not one, but two lambs lying at the feet of their mother, a ewe Sally has named No-Tag in deference to her virgin ears, and to distinguish her from Red-Tag and Yellow-Tag. (Many of her sheep have at some time had plastic tags punched through their ears, leaving them punkishly ragged or perforated.) No-Tag was nudging and licking clean her lambs, one of which must have been born barely five minutes before, and was talking to them in the low, rumbling, phlegmy voice that is unique to ewes with new-born lambs. The children sat on a hurdle, waving the torch beam in all directions, as Sally led the ewe into a pen by dragging the still-wet lambs before her, and uttering a fair imitation of her gravelly tone. Sally sprayed the lambs' navels with a purple antiseptic and drew down some of the ewe's milk, of which she had a generous supply. We left them as the lambs were fighting their rubbery, overlong legs to stand up for the first time. The children went to bed in a state of high excitement, and I was surprised they got to sleep so easily.

Later, when Sally was asleep too, I returned to the garage.

The ewe was still grumbling over them, but they were both upright and when I felt their stomachs they were tight and round, like well-inflated rubber balls, so I knew they were feeding properly. The mother had licked them dry and clean, but their wool was encrusted with the yellow, waxy rind of placenta that protects them when they are first born. As I stood over them, one tottered forward, its tail wriggling, and ducked its head to butt the ewe's udder. The other cried in a puling, monotonous voice, and made occasional lunges at the ewe's shoulder, but apart from these misdirected efforts I could see nothing wrong with it, and I decided to let Sally sleep.

The children are usually sluggish and dull first thing in the morning, requiring cups of tea and a longish spell of preparation in our bed before they are willing to face the day. But this morning, while I was making the tea in the kitchen, I heard Tilly run from her room, along the corridor, and into Jack's room. Next, they both stumbled down the stairs, Jack still hot and confused from sleep, his hair standing up like a coconut's, and they ran out of the house, leaving all the doors open.

They were soon back inside, demanding their breakfast.

'We've given them names. They're called Moonie and Sparkle,' Tilly announced in her most authoritative voice.

Moonie I took to be a reference to its nocturnal birth, rather than to Dr Moon and his cult, but I was surprised by the choice of Sparkle, for that had been the name of one of Sally's very first lambs, an orphan which we hand-fed and took up as a favourite. Tilly, who was only four then, became passionately attached to him, and was badly shocked and upset when he suddenly died of some wasting disease. She mourned for him for many weeks after, often asking about him and mentioning his name for no reason.

During breakfast, Tilly asked if the lambs were to be killed. Sally made an equivocal reply.

'Will they *all* be killed?' she asked again, giving Sally a chance to offer her some genuine comfort.

'Perhaps we'll keep the new Sparkle,' she said, 'because she looks a good lamb and we could breed from her next year.'

Tilly seemed content with this compromise and the subject was dropped. Although they wish it did not have to happen, the children have become used to the fact that lambs are in the end sent for slaughter. This year will no doubt be more painful than previous ones, because they will have spent so much time looking after the lambs, but we cannot protect them from this sadness to come without first depriving them of the pleasure of their attachment.

Two years ago we had another favourite, Johnnie, who was hand-fed and grew into a barrel-bellied mammoth. For some reason he escaped butchering during the summer of his birth and survived into the following spring, growing ever more monstrous. Tilly would only be reconciled to his death after we had agreed to her primitive stipulation that she should be allowed to eat him.

'He must go into my tummy,' she would say, rubbing herself gruesomely.

This cannabilistic form of possession is very curious, and Jack never shared it. Throughout such conversations about the fate of lambs, he always stays silent, but looks very melancholy. I suppose the explanation of her bizarre fantasy is that by ingesting the unfortunate Johnnie she thought she would be perpetuating his existence – his flesh would be intermingled with hers, thus bestowing on him a kind of vicarious immortality.

In the event, he did not enjoy this doubtful after-life, for Tilly had converted to vegetarianism by the time he was fat enough to be slaughtered.

On Non-Smoking Day (12 March), Sally attacked me with

such a barrage of gruesome statistics concerning the fate, not of smokers themselves, but their innocent, non-smoking companions, that I forswore cigarettes on the spot, and have not smoked one for a week now. (Of cigars, I say nothing.) This is by no means my first attempt to abstain, but I feel a stronger sense of commitment than usual, because my consumption had been galloping uncontrollably towards sixty a day, and I had contracted a piercing stitch in my chest, which has only just begun to fade.

All this talk of the lethal effects of cigarettes made me think of my paternal grandmother, Queenie, the only member of her family of heavy smokers whose death could be directly attributed to tobacco. I have no idea how many cigarettes a day she smoked, but she had an ungovernably addictive temperament, which I seem to have inherited in full measure. As a child, I was fascinated by her smoking, for she was very artful at keeping her cigarette between her lips while she talked, and I would watch her mouth, mesmerized by its agile movements which made her cigarette bounce and wag, but never dislodged its elongating tip of grey ash. She never allowed the ash to fall off, but always caught it just before it drooped to breaking point, flicking it with an expert click of her thumbnail into an ashtray. She seemed never to be without a cigarette; indeed, my father remembers how as a small boy he had to be careful to dodge her inevitable cigarette when she gave him a bath, for otherwise he would get burnt as she leaned over to wash him.

In the end, it was her circulatory system that was damaged. She collapsed and was taken to a nursing home, where I visited her and, as a special treat, was shown her blackened feet. I did not understand how this was caused by smoking, and was forced to conclude that she had somehow charred herself. She was of course instructed to stop smoking, but she could not manage to do so altogether. By way of trying to retain a whiff of her old pleasure, she kept an unlit cigarette in her mouth, and in this way consumed twenty or more a day merely by making them soggy. In time, she weakened, as she was bound to, and lit the odd one, then ten a day, and soon she was back to her old punishing rate.

She had another thrombosis while I was away at school. My mother wrote to tell me she was ill, and the next day I went into town and bought her a couple of jigsaw puzzles, which after patience were her favourite form of solitary amusement. My parcel arrived the day she died, though I believe it was opened for her and she understood what it contained and who had sent it. My mother wrote me a gentle letter, telling me of her death, and that it had been decided there was no need for me to attend her cremation. I do not remember having strong feelings about this, one way or the other, but I was puzzled nevertheless by their decision. I do not criticize my parents, who were only respecting my grandfather's wish that the least possible 'fuss' should be made. Her death had destroyed his life, and he wanted to grieve alone and unwatched.

On the other hand, as a matter of general principle, I believe children should be allowed, in fact should be made, to attend funerals and cremations. The present middle-class vogue for plain, unceremonious funerals, and worse still for dispensing with ceremony altogether, strikes me as unhealthy and sad, a sign of our culture's confusion in the face of death, which leaves the individual isolated and protected by neither myth nor social ritual. I myself wish to be buried with all the pomp and circumstance my family can afford: I envisage muffled drums, black-plumed horses, a polished oak coffin glittering with brass fixtures, and bare-headed villagers lining the street as an endless cortège slow-marches towards the church yard; I envisage graveside orations, lorry-loads of priceless flowers, crowds too big to be accommodated in the church and, most important of all, a tombstone of positively vulgar magnificence.

Although I am quite sincere in wanting my death to be marked and honoured, I am able to write in this flippant vein because I am lucky enough to have reached the age of forty-two without having yet suffered real grief. The deaths of all my grandparents saddened me, but only briefly, and never caused me any pain. However, I still believe that people need ritual to give them a formal opportunity to express their grief, and to give tangible finality to the life of the person being buried. It is not just vanity that prompts me to want an ostentatious funeral, but a longing for all those rites of passage which help us make sense of existence and our own mysterious coming and going.

To my mind, this is another reason for encouraging our children to have the closest involvement with Sally's sheep — not that they need any encouragement. Over the years, they have been able to watch the cycle of life and death continually fulfilling and renewing itself. Sally has owned one of her ewes for more than five seasons now, and that is longer than Jack's memory, and probably Tilly's too. Some of her ewes have been sold and replaced; some have died and we have watched their bodies being dragged away by the local hunt to be fed to their hounds; some have been sold locally and are still visited. Only yesterday, the children went to call on 'Sweetie', an elderly ewe once owned by Sally, which allows the children to hug and hang on her unless she has lambs, whereupon she gives the lie to her name and turns into a tigress, or at least a passable sheep-imitation of one. Most of their lambs are sold for slaughter, but some are kept because they fail to achieve a marketable weight, or because they might make good breeders themselves. However, as far as the children are concerned, these events, and the decisions that cause them, are as arbitrary as fate. Sally's decisions are of course far from arbitrary, being determined mostly by economics, but to the children they are both inexplicable and unacceptable, just as the workings of destiny, and its principles, are inscrutable and hateful to us. The children are not consulted, nor are their wishes respected, for if they had their way, not a single lamb or ewe would ever be sold, far less killed. In this respect, Sally behaves like a wilful, careless god, playing with life and death for her sport and amusement. The children must therefore come to terms with these events by using their own resources and understanding, which in effect amounts to developing a sense of emotional balance. And this can only stand them in good stead, for who knows when our turn to be culled will come?

I also think it important that they get to touch, as well as watch these processes. They have felt the oil-drum bellies of the ewes as they reach the full term of their pregnancy; they have prodded the slimy coats of new-born lambs with a shrinking finger; they have held the greedy heads of orphan lambs and pushed bottles into their mouths, and they have discovered how the fluffy, shampooed curls of lambs' wool turns into the thick, lanolin-clogged fleece of a mature sheep. As a result, they know that meat is not made in factories in neat, square-shaped lumps, and they know that wool is not an invention of Marks and Spencer. They have been brought that much closer to the living texture of existence, from which our civilization is forever threatening to separate us.

Even country people have been put at a distance from these elemental processes of growth, for nowadays to live within sight of a farm is no guarantee of having any contact with its plants and animals. The average East Anglian child is surrounded by rolling grain prairies in summer and whole parishes of potatoes and sugar beet in winter, and he may even glimpse the occasional pig in a paddock, but none of this means that he has any more first-hand experience of farming or nature than the average East End child. Farming has become a highly specialized industry, occupying a tiny handful of people, whose work, though highly visible, is unintelligible to the onlooking public as it drives through the countryside. We see, but we no longer understand, and we certainly very seldom touch. The effect of this alienation from the seasonal cycles and the processes of birth and growth is to take away our respect for life itself, and by extension for tradition, for anything that needs time, security and care to reach maturity and fulfil its inborn promise. This alienation also sharpens our appetite for the new and ephemeral, for things that have no history and sensations that are instant and narcotic; it hardens our impatience with relationships that are problematic and require years, not just days, to repair; and it excites the casual destructiveness that is becoming an everyday feature of our relations, both on the street and at home.

And so it was that my grandmother was cremated in my absence. Her remains must, I suppose, have been buried or deposited somewhere, but it is only now, as I write this, that I realize, with a shock, that I have no idea where she lies buried, or if indeed there is any monument to her and her husband, who died many years later. For her sake and mine, I wish I had been brought home to attend her cremation. Her memory deserved to be honoured, especially by someone to whom she had given nothing but pleasure. And I, for my part, would not have felt so cut off from my emotions if, as a general rule, I had been given the chance to express them, and they had not been seen as something from which I had to be protected. I must have felt grief for Queenie, but it never surfaced; instead, it was driven underground to swell the lava boiling beneath my cracked and friable crust.

Every day of March brings spring closer, and puts November further behind us. There are still no leaves on the trees and no wild flowers to be seen, apart from snowdrops, but the weather has lost its wintry edge and the light is acquiring that crystalline clarity which is a sure signal of spring. Sally's lambing yard, with its straw-bale walls and mangers full of hay, to say nothing of its inmates, is providing a perfect builder's yard for the birds which have begun to nest, and the view from my window is constantly criss-crossed by chaffinches, tits and sparrows rushing to and fro, carrying stalks and little hanks of wool. The lambs themselves are of course the most unmistakable and exhilarating symbol of spring. Yesterday afternoon, Sally put out her flock to eat the grass in the garden and it made a classic, if eccentric, picture: the sun shone in a blue sky, a few freshly laundered white clouds rolled by, and the first daffodils fluttered and danced in the breeze. The lambs themselves, as if eager to complete this clichéd scene, gambolled and skipped. It would take a very jaded eye to resist the charm of these 'jocund' creatures: they do indeed seem to frisk and sport for the sheer joy of being alive. The very earth seems to shoot some electrifying charge of vitality into their limbs, making them quiver and wriggle in an ecstasy of high spirits.

During the March following Jack's birth, Sally and I took the first steps towards recovering our old physical selves. As it happened, the first step was forced on Sally, because by then Jack had pulverized her into such a state of tenderness that she could not continue to feed him. Despite feeling that she ought to persist, she rang our doctor who advised her to give up this self-inflicted torture and prescribed some pills to suppress her milk. However, they did not take effect immediately, and for two excruciating days Sally's breasts ballooned, fountained and hardened to the consistency of coconuts. It seemed that they must burst, but at last the pressure subsided and Sally began to resume her old shape. Jack, meanwhile, was quite content to exchange the breast for a bottle, and mother's milk for cow's.

Tilly had been weaned a little later, but under dramatic circumstances. On her first Boxing Day, when she was about three and a half months old, we were driving back from Woodbridge along an obscure and narrow lane when we were suddenly struck by another car. Tilly, lying in her basket in the back of our Mini-Traveller, took a blow on the head and screamed. I staggered out to talk to the other driver and inspect the damage. As the man was making his ludicrous excuses for being on the wrong side of the road, Sally ran from the back of our car, brandishing Tilly like a claymore, and threatened to kill him. It was a dreadful day for all of us, but it did have one happy outcome in that Sally's milk dried up on the spot.

Apart from the brief interval between Tilly's dramatic weaning and Jack's conception, Sally had not been able to call her body her own for more than two years, and I, who had previously been used to enjoying it freely, had been competing with embryos and babies. Once her milk had finally stopped flowing, which took all of six days, we asked the doctor when we could take up our sex life again. We were told we could look forward to 'marital relations' in a fortnight's time. For the second time, I wrote 'Hurrah' in my diary. Sally envied me my unmarked body, feeling that her own had been shattered and damaged by the birth and nursing of two children, while I was conscious of not having held her, with the liberty to touch her as I pleased, for too many months.

When Sally was pregnant with Tilly we did make love occasionally and with pleasure, though we did so less and less towards the end, but with Jack we stopped almost as soon as she knew she was pregnant again. As with many of the decisions affecting the most intimate aspects of our marriage, this one was made by mutual consent, but tacitly, without much discussion, if any. By then I had of course seen Tilly being born and neither of us associated childbirth, and therefore pregnancy itself, with any kind of sexual interest. For the mother, no matter how rewarding she finds the overall experience, there is bound to be an element of sexual humiliation involved in giving birth, for her most private self is not only exposed, but gorily distorted and mauled. Watching this voluntary and wished-for violence is disturbing for the father too. Even if he finds childbirth a fulfilling and exhilarating experience, as most do, it may still leave a residue of fear and horror, which is only registered later when a new pregnancy revives memories of an earlier ordeal. At any rate, so it was with me.

During Tilly's birth I felt nothing but excitement and pride, but when it came to Jack's turn I reacted very differently. I remember seeing Sally's swollen, purple body with Jack's head, a slimy patch of black scalp, just visible. Then there was a sudden convulsion as his head emerged, followed by the quick slither of his entire body gliding out, a reddened fish-child crusted with white, waxy scales, which the midwife netted in a towel. He was already crying. A tumult of relief and happiness overwhelmed me, but I was also sickened by the punishment Sally had taken, and as the long twisted cable of his umbilical cord spilled out I had to look away and put my head between my knees.

The vagina is, after all, the ultimate focus of sexual desire and activity, but during childbirth it is required to do things that are the very antithesis of sexiness. Ordinarily, the vagina – a word that conjures up none of its loving and loveable connotations – is a centre of warmth, excitation and bliss. To the male mind, it suggests the final homecoming of pleasure, the active recipient of desire, the object and subject of passion, the point of union, the root of transcendence, the haven of self-forgetfulness, the cauldron of ecstasy, the couch of tranquillity. But whatever fantasies are suggested, its essential sexual function is to admit and embrace, whereas in childbirth the opposite is the case, for then it contracts and discharges, expelling, rather than receiving life. Instead of the outer penetrating the inner, instead of one organ swelling and stretching to enfold another, the inside is thrust out, everything is bent towards eviction, and the avenue of pleasure becomes a turnpike of pain. In a certain sense, there is an analogy with orgasm, inasmuch as birth too continually approaches a crescendo; but no one would undertake the experience for its own sake; and the sensual pleasure of childbirth, to which some mothers do lay claim, is strictly incidental. There is certainly little in the way of sensual pleasure for the onlooking father, who more than anything is conscious of the painful battering, and its bloody consequences, being inflicted on a part he had hitherto thought of as special to him, and precious for its tender delights. To see it mangled and bludgeoned is a shocking sight, and one that must leave its mark on later sexual responses, if only in the short term.

I know I am writing in a histrionic vein, but outside the delivery room, it is not easy to describe these emotions in cold blood, as it were, and conjure up the hysteria that grips the helpless father, without resorting to what may sound like exaggerated language. Perhaps I am only disclosing my own unconscious fears, but in any event I would be surprised to hear of any couple who, after childbirth attended by the father, blithely returned to their old way of love-making and felt no change of feeling, either for each other or in themselves.

When the fortnight had elapsed and we had our chance to make love again, to which we had been looking forward with ever-increasing impatience, the outcome was farcical and disastrous. We chose to use the sheath as our means of contraception, but at the appropriate moment we were terrified to see a lurid green thing uncoil itself from the foil sachet where it had lain cocooned, like some grotesque insect. A revolution had evidently taken place in the design of French letters, for when I last opened one, fifteen or more years before, it had been pink, a skin sloughed off by a human-coloured snake. Not realizing that we now lived in a more colourful world, and thinking that we had perhaps hit on a faulty one, we opened another sachet, only to be confronted by an electric-blue device, which glowed with radioactive malevolence. The third in the packet turned out to be a glistening black, more reminiscent of plastic refuse bags than any erotic, human quality. Taking our courage in both hands, as it were, we elected to use the original swamp-green one, but had been too distracted to enjoy ourselves. And then, to our horror, as passion subsided, our protector simply fell off inside Sally, and the possibility of her being pregnant again was suddenly with us in the bed, dividing us like a sword. It was not until that moment that either of us fully realized how desperate we were not to have another child, at least in the immediate future. Despite having adopted a belt-and-braces policy by using a spermicidal cream as well as our rainbow rubbers, we were too nervous to take the risk a second time and we decided to wait another fortnight when Sally would be able to start a new course of the pill.

This unfortunate event was not only frustrating, but humiliating, and for the first time in our sexual relationship Sally and I felt estranged from each other. We had always enjoyed a carefree, companionable sex life, but now, without any change in our emotions to cause it, sex had suddenly become a problem, a source of anxiety and dissatisfaction, and its poison began to seep into our ordinary, everyday behaviour. I soon came to feel that I had to restrain myself from making affectionate gestures to Sally, especially physical ones, for fear of having to stifle them and put up with more disappointment. Such is the perverse logic set in motion by sexual discord, I also came to feel that the situation was Sally's fault, that she was not resenting our enforced celibacy as keenly as I, and that if she had really wanted sex, she could have done something to make it possible.

Our fear of pregnancy and our ignominious failure to master the most primitive of contraceptive shields, which any drunken teenager could use, certainly had its inhibiting effect and placed a strain on us that was all the harder to bear for being new to our marriage. But on my side there was another constraint, which was impossible to discuss with Sally and almost impossible to acknowledge to myself, and that was my reluctance, despite an ever-sharpening frustration, to re-enter Sally's body after watching the beating it took during Jack's delivery. I found Sally herself as attractive as ever – more so, owing to our long, enforced abstinence – but now there was no longer a simple equation between desire and satisfaction. Too many complications stood in the way, and our old unworried spontaneity, which is the key to successful sex, had been banished. Although I did not articulate it explicitly at the time, either to Sally or myself, I think I was terrified of her getting pregnant again partly because of a guilty sense of being responsible myself for her ordeal. I felt that her pain would be the price of my pleasure.

Looking back, I also think that the traumatic impact of his delivery affected my attitude to Jack, delaying my acceptance of him by quite a few months. He was of course utterly innocent, but one's mind, especially when under the combined influence of guilt and sexual confusion, does not always work rationally, and in some remote, unexamined corner of my thinking I held him to blame, along with myself, for the hurt Sally suffered at his birth. Writing today from a distance of more than seven years, I can still see that dreadful scene in the delivery suite with all its original clarity, but it no longer connects with the real Sally of the present day, and its effect is now inseparably mixed into the general stew of experience. However, for a while, it overshadowed our emotional life in ways that were as difficult to identify as to understand.

In the event, it was not until the end of April, nearly a month and a half on, before we made another attempt at sex. By then Sally had been fitted with a coil, so we had no technological difficulties to overcome, and we were beginning to free ourselves from the anxieties that weigh down all parents with new-born babies. Jack was that much older, and his grasp on life now seemed secure, and Tilly had cheerfully adapted to his presence in her life. And so, when one Sunday afternoon Tilly fell asleep over her lunch, leaving Jack contentedly drowsing in his basket, we eyed each other and decided not to waste the opportunity. The afternoon had always been our favoured time, and our nervousness was allayed by the effects of a roast lunch and red wine. We took the children upstairs to their room, which connected with ours, and went to bed ourselves.

The afternoon was balmy and peaceful: we could hear the deep-rolling snores of the sows beneath our window, as they digested their lunchtime feed. The first flies of the year sizzled on the hot glass, while the sunshine warmed our bed and bathed beautiful Sally in a pool of yellow light. The farm outside slumbered in Sunday quiet, our children inside breathed gently in their sleep, and at last our domestic world seemed to have slipped into a restful harmony.

Soon enough, Sally and I also fell into a dreamless, satisfied sleep.

The worst gale for a decade blew up yesterday. In our part of the country these winds are all the more terrifying and destructive because they meet with no obstacles, but sweep unhindered across the flat, hedgeless fields, driving a dust-storm before them and leaving behind a battered landscape skinned of its topsoil. The ash trees in the wood behind us fired off a continual fusillade of twigs and small branches; the Scots pine beside Jack's hole, whose trunk despite its drunken lean is usually as motionless as a cast-iron column, was bouncing and heaving; the pantile roof on our barn billowed like a loosened toupee; and Sally could only get to her sheep by putting her head down and butting through the gusts with the action of an ice-breaker. At midday the electricity failed and I had to resort to my manual typewriter, whose keys need hitting so hard I felt as if I were engraving the letters on tablets of stone.

The winds raged and the world outside shredded apart, but inside a still more violent tempest blew, for Sally and I had our worst row since November. We were suddenly overtaken by a terrible fury, which ripped through us and shook the very joists and rafters of our marriage. We shouted and slammed doors, we cursed and abused each other, we hurled bitterness and hatred round the kitchen, we roared and howled. But like the storm outside, this was no ordinary quarrel: it was an equinoctial, the signal that a new season was upon us, that spring had at last joined battle with winter, which would soon be banished to its ice-bound retreat. For the first time since my homecoming from Norfolk we were daring to fight; though we did not say so, we knew we could clash now without demolishing everything we had pieced together over the last four months. Sally felt free to release the tornado of rage that had been swelling inside her all this time, and for my part I was no longer so inhibited by guilt that I felt unable to answer her back.

During the afternoon the wind outside strengthened, but we had to put our private cyclone back in its bottle when the children returned from school. Far from being frightened by the storm, they appeared to be intoxicated and were full of bloodcurdling stories of killer slates flying through the air and slicing people's heads off. Stimulated perhaps by the candles and oil-lamps we had to light, they decided to dress up. Tilly presented herself as a princess, easily identifiable by her white tablecloth cape and cardboard crown, but Jack's disguise, though more elaborate, was harder to label. He was wearing the grey school blazer he once bought at a jumble sale and has used as the basis of innumerable uniforms and transformations. From its breast pocket a silk handkerchief flowed, together with the chain of my pocket watch, which he hauled out and consulted with a great show of scientific precision, noting down the time, quite erroneously, in one of the many notebooks bulging from his other pockets. Followed by a pirhouetting Tilly, he stalked round the shadowy kitchen peering at objects through a large magnifying glass.

'What are you doing?'

'Inspecting.'

Of course! Here was Sherlock Holmes to the life. We have never read him a Holmes story and he really has no idea who or what Holmes is, but he has picked up the name and identified with it, for he loves anything that smacks of crime-busting. They are both fascinated by the seeming magic of detective work and have become ardent fans of Agatha Christie adaptations for television.

They departed, hot on the trail of some clue, but returned shortly afterwards, Tilly having abandoned her royal robes and now wearing her own blazer, a cherry red affair with brass buttons.

'Who are you?' I asked her.

'Miss Marbles. Who do you think?' she replied in her most scathing tone.

That night the Great Detective and his female counterpart went to bed very contentedly by the light of an oil-lamp at an absurdly early hour. The absence of electricity seemed to disorient them, and as soon as it was completely dark outside they were ready for sleep.

During the night, which was almost as wild as the day had been, one of Sally's oldest ewes, known as 'Prolapse', gave birth to twins, and despite her name and history, did so without difficulty, needing no help from Sally or her friend who had come to stay in the hope of seeing a lamb born. We all went to look at them in the morning. These were truly children of the storm. Everywhere around them the devastation was appalling, but they were already tottering confidently through the straw and butting their aged mother's udder to bring down her milk. Our wood appeared to have been ravaged by an army of hooligans which had torn off all the vulnerable branches and chucked them across the paths. Surprisingly, only one complete tree had been blown over, an ash, which turned out to be rotten at the roots. We were lucky, for the beautiful avenue of trees that leads down to Stowlangtoft Hall was a sad sight, having lost four beeches and a lime.

The wind still gusted, but only in a casual, off-handed way, its destructiveness spent. After our enforced lull, Sally and I allowed our storm to revive, yet it too had blown itself out. I was cool with Sally until the children had gone to school, then we bickered for a while, but with none of yesterday's intensity, and by lunchtime we were once more on amicable, affection-ate terms. I now believe that our dreadful winter is on the retreat as surely as the natural one outside; ours, however, is a season that will never return – at least, I devoutly hope so. There will no doubt be cold snaps in our relationship, even the odd fall of snow and attack of frost, but we will never again allow ourselves to be overtaken and frozen up by another glacial winter. We are liberated forever from the ice-age I brought down on our house in November.

After school, I took the children for a walk through the

wood. The sky was a friendly brawl of clear blue and white cloud, riven by the squally winds that still shook the crowns of the trees and made the brittle ash branches rattle together. A wreckage of twigs and broken boughs littered the ground in a loose mat, but beneath the rubble we discovered new life springing up everywhere. Little spikes and prickets of green tissue were shooting through the leaf mould, the most common being the tips of dog's mercury, which in less than a month's time will cover the wood floor in large, dense stands. It was a curious sensation to walk on a surface which for the last six months has been little more than mud, grass and rotting leaves, knowing that this dormant turf had suddenly been charged with fresh vitality and was bursting at every pore with vegetable energy. The earth was crunchy with life, and we hesitated to put down our feet for fear of crushing the filaments of growth which were invisible from our height, but close to could be seen oozing and uncoiling from the loam. The chestnut leaves had already begun to explode from the gummy grasp of their buds, and yet this early shimmer of green did nothing to indicate the vast tonnage of leaf and flower that will shortly gush from the branches and leap from the floor when the whole wood rises to the call of spring.

When we returned to the house, we found Sally with her sheep, which she had just put out to graze on the lawn. So far she has had nine lambs from five of her ewes, and they are now old enough to join up in a gang and play together. They ran from one end of the lawn to the other, frisking and leaping. They jumped on the straw bales put out to give them shelter, they jumped on their long-suffering mothers, they fought mock battles, butting and stamping, they leapt into the air and broke away from their games to punch their mothers' udders with their noses, wriggling their tails as they tasted the milk. The children ran to the kitchen to get a bucket of vegetable scraps and fed them, leaf by leaf, to the greedy mouths that pushed their way through the electrified netting. The ram fought for his share as eagerly as the rest, though he usually remains aloof from the activities of his expanding family. He takes no interest in his offspring, who likewise ignore him, and he appears not to have retained even a glimmer of instinctive protectiveness, for he leaves every aspect of the lambs' nurturing and upbringing to his ewes.

We, however, were a united family. We stood together, Sally and I arm in arm, the children burrowing into our coats for warmth against the evening chill, and looked back towards the darkening wood to watch a last flock of pigeons wheel in from the field and take up their roost for the night.

Our winter's tale was done.

Flamingo

Flamingo is a quality imprint publishing both fiction and non-fiction. Below are some recent titles.

Fiction
- [ ] The House on Moon Lake *Francesca Durante* £3.50
- [ ] The Blacksmith's Daughter *Shaun Herron* £3.50
- [ ] The Red Men *Patrick McGinley* £3.95
- [ ] The Pale Sergeant *James Murray* £3.50
- [ ] Liberation of Margaret McCabe *Catherine Brophy* £3.50
- [ ] Mating Birds *Lewis Nkosi* £3.50
- [ ] Lady's Time *Alan Hewat* £3.95
- [ ] The Mind and Body Shop *Frank Parkin* £3.50
- [ ] Perfect English *Paul Pickering* £3.50

Non-fiction
- [ ] Rain or Shine *Cyra McFadden* £3.50
- [ ] Love is Blue *Joan Wyndham* £3.50
- [ ] Love Lessons *Joan Wyndham* £2.95

You can buy Flamingo paperbacks at your local bookshop or newsagent. Or you can order them from Fontana Paperbacks, Cash Sales Department, Box 29, Douglas, Isle of Man. Please send a cheque, postal or money order (not currency) worth the purchase price plus 22p per book (or plus 22p per book if outside the UK).

NAME (Block letters) _____

ADDRESS_____

_____

_____